STUDENT'S BOOK

Framework

LEVEL **2**

BEN GOLDSTEIN

www.webframework.net

Contents

Reading	Speaking	Writing	Pronunciation	Takeaway English
Person and city profiles 'London: multicultural capital of the world' Promotional texts	Interviewing a partner Describing your city Talking about films and famous cities	A short text about a classmate 'Sell your town' – an advert	/b/ and /v/	Giving directions
'Close encounters' 'Are you a true friend?' questionnaire Short text about *Friends*	Discussing physical appearances Talking about how people meet each other Describing personal changes	A love story from picture prompts A soap opera **WORKBOOK** Writing stories	/ʃ/	Chatting up
Web page about job candidates 'Stress test' 'Rat race rebels' Short job adverts and application letter	Hypothesising about jobs Discussing stressful situations Discussing job interviews	A job application letter	/j/ and /dʒ/	A job interview
Article: Nike and Umbro 'Thorpedo!'	Discussing favourite sports Giving views on controversial sports	'Expressing your opinions' – a composition **WORKBOOK** Writing about an interest	/n/ and /ŋ/ Connected speech	Joining a gym
'A weekend in Lisbon with Sunshine Tours' '15 months that can change your life' Postcards and e-mails	Discussing holidays Talking about gap years Practising making decisions	A postcard	Contractions with *will* /l/	Booking a hotel
'Are you a junk food freak?' questionnaire 'Chocoholics' Article: *The Big Diet* TV programme	Discussing addictions Interviewing an addict Giving advice about health and other problems	A recipe **WORKBOOK** Writing about your opinions	/uː/ and /ʊ/	Ordering food

4

Reading	Speaking	Writing	Pronunciation	Takeaway English
'Are you mean with money?' Company histories Article about anti-globalisation	Discussing market leaders and globalisation Analysing and describing adverts	An advert	/ɒ/ and /ʌ/	Money problems
Biographical texts Short newspaper articles 'Who's got the gossip?'	Discussing celebrities Giving opinions about the sensationalist press Defining gossip	A news story **WORKBOOK** A profile of a film star	/h/	Gossiping
'Kidults' 'You and your messages' quiz	Talking about time saved and wasted with new technology Discussing pros and cons of mobile phones Talking about websites, the internet and chat rooms	Writing instructions	'd and 'll /ai/	Telephoning: business or pleasure?
Article about Spanglish 'Languages in danger' An advert	Discussing life abroad Analysing small talk Asking and answering quiz questions Ranking ideas for teaching and language learning	Quiz questions **WORKBOOK** Writing about advantages and disadvantages	/tʃ/ and /k/	Class language
Short descriptions of people's clothes 'Test your personality' colour quiz 'Are you a fashion victim?'	Talking about changes of image Describing personality Talking about fashion	Writing sentences on changes of look A description of an item of clothing A class survey	/ʃ/ and /ʒ/	Clothes shopping
'Cars – curse or craze?' 'The young and angry: in their own words' '2050 – A day in the life of Citizen KYZ606' 'Future homes'	Discussing pros and cons of cars Talking about stories in the news Making predictions about the future	A diary **WORKBOOK** Writing a letter to a newspaper	/juː/ and /ʌ/	Future plans

1 The concrete jungle

- Present Simple & Past Simple
- Questions
- City adjectives
- Compound nouns
- /b/ & /v/
- Giving directions

My town

Speaking & Reading

1 **Answer the questions.**

1 Where are you from?
2 Do you like cities?
3 Do you live in the place where you were born?
4 If not, why did you move?

2 **Read the texts. Are these sentences true (T) or false (F)? If false, explain why.**

1 Everybody's parents have different nationalities.
   F – Rashid's parents are both from India.
2 Everybody likes cities.
3 Linda likes her job.
4 Carolina is the most positive about her city.
5 Rashid was born in Bombay.

3 **Complete these sentences with the correct name.**

1 _____ doesn't work.
2 _____ can speak the most languages.
3 _____ thinks that the city helps him / her to be creative.

Carolina

Hi, I'm Carolina and I'm 21 years old. I live in Berlin, but I was born in the south of Italy. We moved here from Italy when I was 14 because of my father's work. I'm half German, half Italian. I started working in the family business a few years ago – we have a jewellers' shop. I work in the shop every afternoon except Sundays, but it's a bit boring. The city is OK but I never have time to enjoy it – everything is so hectic. I often miss Italy.

Rashid

My name's Rashid. I'm 24 and I live in London. I'm Indian, but I was born here in the UK. My parents came here from Bombay (we call it Mumbai now) at the end of the 1960s. London's a great place to be for me because I study architecture and there are lots of interesting buildings around. Every day I see something new. I don't want to live anywhere else.

Linda

My name's Linda. I'm 25 and live in a small town outside Vancouver. My mother is Spanish and my father comes from Lagos in Nigeria. We speak English, French and Spanish at home. I work as a teacher in the local school. It's a great job but very tiring because I get up very early every morning. Before, I worked as a secretary – I didn't like it at all! I really like the town I live in, although it's very cold in winter. Cities like Vancouver are just too big for me.

Vocabulary
City adjectives

1 Underline the adjectives in the texts on page 6. Which are:

a) positive   b) negative   c) neutral?

EXAMPLE: boring – negative

2 Are these adjectives positive or negative in your opinion?

cosmopolitan   crowded   dirty   dynamic   noisy   polluted
sophisticated   stressful   touristy   ugly   varied   welcoming

3 Which of the adjectives could you use to describe your city or town?

Language focus
Present Simple and
Past Simple

1 Circle the verbs in the texts on page 6. Are they in the Present Simple or Past Simple tense?

2 Look at the photo of Rita. What nationality do you think she is?

3 🎧(1.1) Listen and complete the text with verbs in the Present Simple or Past Simple.

Rita

Hi there, I'm Rita. I ¹<u>was born</u> in Jamaica, but my family ² _____ to Paris when I ³ _____ two years old. We ⁴ _____ our own business a few years ago and it's going very well. I ⁵ _____ Paris because there ⁶ _____ so much to do and see. It's impossible to get bored. The only problem is everything ⁷ _____ a fortune.

Present Simple

I **work** in the shop every afternoon.
I **study** architecture.

We use the Present Simple to talk about **routines** and **facts**.

Find three more examples from the texts on page 6.

....
....
....

I **don't work** in the shop in the morning.
My father **doesn't live** in Bombay now.

To make the Present Simple **negative**, we use the auxiliary .... / .... + verb.

Past Simple

I **worked** as a secretary.   They **moved** here in the 1960s.

We use the Past Simple to talk about a finished **state** or **action** in the past.

Find three more examples from the texts on page 6.

....
....
....

I **didn't like** my first job.

To make the Past Simple **negative**, we use the auxiliary .... + verb.

See Reference Guide, pp. 2–3.
See Workbook, pp. 3–4, exs 1–4.

Practice

Are these sentences true (T) or false (F) for you and where you live? If false, make the sentences true.

1 Most people work from 9 am to 5 pm.
   F – Most people don't work from 9 am to 5 pm. They work from 9 am to 7 pm.
2 The streets are often very noisy.
3 Eating out is expensive.
4 Most people travel around by car.
5 My parents were born here.
6 I liked the city more when I was a child.

Speaking & Writing

1 Interview your partner using these prompts.

1 What / name? What's your name?   4 Where / born?
2 How / old?   5 When / arrive / (place)?
3 What / do?   6 Do / like / the city? Why / Why not?

2 Write a short text about your partner from memory. Then swap texts with your partner. Is the text about him / her correct?

Ethnic communities

Speaking & Reading

1 Look at these pictures. Which ones do you associate with England? Why?

2 Which nationalities would you expect to find in London?

3 Work in pairs.

Student A: Read texts A, B, C. **Student B:** Read texts D, E, F.

Match the communities to the places on the London map.

4 Student A: Turn to page 118. **Student B:** Turn to page 120.

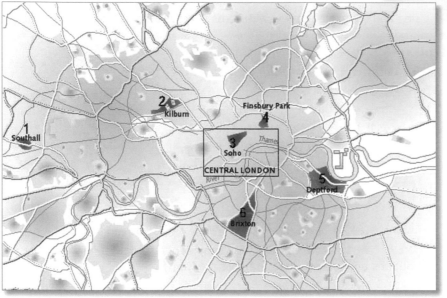

5 Discuss these questions.

1 What surprised you about the article on London?

2 Are there any ethnic communities living in your town / city?

LONDON:

MULTICULTURAL CAPITAL OF THE WORLD

London is one of the most multicultural cities in the world, with about 300 different cultures living side by side. Forget tea and sandwiches, now it is more common for a Londoner to drink cappuccino for breakfast, and eat Thai food for lunch in the local pub. Let's see how life has changed in Britain's capital.

A India

Most people from India arrived in London in the 1950s and 60s. Now there is a strong Asian presence here – in the shops, markets and, of course, the restaurants. In fact, curry is Britain's favourite takeaway meal. A typical family has a curry every two weeks, either delivered or bought ready-made from the supermarket. Indian people live all over London. Southall, in the west of the city, is one of many places well known for its Indian culture.

B Greece

The bars and cafés near Finsbury Park in north-east London are a clear sign that you are in 'Little Athens'. Here, there is a really cosmopolitan atmosphere – people are always in the streets and some of the shops stay open all night. People with a sweet tooth love the traditional cakes and pastries – they're delicious. Today there are almost 300,000 people of Greek and Cypriot origin living in the city.

Try the internet activities for this unit at www.webframework.net.

Language focus
Questions

Word order

Look at the examples and complete the rules.

Are they Greek?
Was your mother from Nigeria?
In questions with the verb ...., we put the subject after the verb.

Do you live in London?
Does Carolina work in a jewellers'?
In **Present Simple questions**, we use the auxiliary .... or .... before the subject.

Did she move to London?
Did they leave India in the 1950s?
In **Past Simple questions**, we use the auxiliary .... before the subject.

Question words

When did they arrive in London?
Where are you from?

After question words, the word order follows the same rules.

Complete the gaps with question words.

.... does the Carnival take place?
.... do the shops in 'Little Athens' stay open?
.... area do a lot of Nigerians live in?
.... food do many London markets sell?

Subject and object questions

Complete the gaps.

1 If *Who, What* or *Which* ask about the **subject**, we replace the subject with the question word and the word order doesn't change.

EXAMPLES:

Which group of people arrived in London in 1885?
    subject
The Chinese arrived in London in 1885.
          subject
.... *lives in London? Rashid lives in London.*

2 If *Who, What* or *Which* ask about the **object**, we put the auxiliary verb before the subject.

EXAMPLES:
          object
What does Rashid study? He studies architecture.

> *See Reference Guide, p. 3.*
> *See Workbook, p. 4, exs 5–7.*

Practice

1 Can you remember? Make questions from the prompts. Answer them.

1 who / move / Berlin / she / 14?
  Who moved to Berlin when she was 14? Carolina.
2 who / study / architecture?
3 when / Rashid / parents / move / London?
4 when / Carolina / work / shop?
5 who / speak / three languages?
6 what / Linda / do / before / she / teacher?

2 Which are subject questions?

C West Africa

West Africans – mainly from Ghana and Nigeria – have brought a wealth of languages, music and culture to the British capital. Many London markets sell their traditional foods like yams and different types of rice. A lot of Nigerians live in the south-east London area, in suburbs like Deptford.

D China

Chinese people first came to Britain in 1885. The first arrivals were mostly seamen. They worked on steamships. In the 1950s, many Chinese people settled in the central Soho area of London and opened restaurants. This area is called Chinatown. Here, you can find the best Chinese restaurants in London and you can buy Chinese vegetables, herbal medicines and gifts.

E The Caribbean

During the 1950s, people from the Caribbean islands (for example, Jamaica and Barbados) arrived in London to start a new life. Their reggae music, steel drums and culture are all now part of the capital's atmosphere, especially during the Notting Hill Carnival. This takes place every August and is Europe's largest and most vibrant street party. One of the centres of the Caribbean community is in Brixton, in the south of London.

F Ireland

The Irish community is the largest in London. They come from all over Ireland – north and south. The largest neighbourhood is Kilburn in north-west London. London has always attracted artists and musicians, and Irish bands and folk singers perform in pubs all over the city.

Then and now

Vocabulary
Compound nouns

1 Match a word in column A with a word in column B to form compound nouns.

A	B
1 shopping	a) store
2 department	b) block
3 tower	c) park
4 traffic	d) road
5 industrial	e) centre
6 sports	f) centre
7 theme	g) estate
8 ring	h) jam

2 Which of these things can you find in your town / city?

Listening

1 🎧1.2 Listen to Jacquie talking about life in London now and five years ago. Tick the things she talks about.

1 offices   4 nightclubs
2 traffic ✔   5 shops
3 restaurants and bars   6 flats

2 Listen again. What has changed? Which changes are:

a) positive?   b) negative?

EXAMPLE: more cars and traffic jams – negative

3 Which words from Vocabulary, above, does Jacquie mention?

EXAMPLE: traffic jam

4 How has your town / city changed over the past five years?

The Real Thing: *a bit (of)* ...

1 🎧1.3 Listen to Jacquie again. How many times do you hear the phrase *a bit*?

2 Listen again. With what other words does she use *a bit*? Complete the gaps.

a bit _____
a bit of a _____
a bit _____

To soften opinion, we can use *a bit* to modify adjectives and *a bit of a* to modify nouns. *A bit* and *a bit of a* ... are often used with negative words.

3 🎧1.4 Listen and complete the gaps. Where do you think the speakers are?

1 No. It's a bit _____.
2 Sorry, she's a bit _____.
3 Can't you clean it up? It's a bit of a _____.
4 You're a bit of a _____, aren't you?

Speaking

What do you like / dislike about your city? Try to use *a bit* in your answers.

EXAMPLE: Madrid's a bit crowded.

Listening

1 Which city in the world would you most like to visit? Which would you least like to visit? Why?

2 (1.5) Listen to Imogen, David, Frank and Laura. What cities are they describing? What words helped you decide?

Imogen – New York (Manhattan ...)

Match the photos (a–d) with the cities.

3 Listen again. Which speakers are:
  1 in the city now?
  2 going to visit the city in the future?
  3 talking about a visit in the past?

4 Which of these adjectives does each person use?

> beautiful   crowded   difficult   exotic
> friendly   helpful   impossible   incredible
> interesting   ~~lively~~   nice   sophisticated

EXAMPLE: Imogen – lively

5 What does each person think of the city?

Speaking

1 Guess the city. Look at the example.

A: I am in a big square. I can see a cathedral with towers of many different colours. It's very cold. Where am I?
B: Moscow?
A: That's right!

2 Work in pairs. Think of a city. Describe where you are. Include a building, a famous landmark and the weather in your description.

Pronunciation

/b/ and /v/

1 (1.6) Listen to the city names. Write them down.

EXAMPLE: Bombay

2 Turn to Reference Guide, page 38, and check your answers in transcript 1.6.

3 Practise saying these words.

pub   river   mobile   glove   lively   carnival
movie   vibrant

4 (1.7) Listen and repeat.

Fact or film?

Speaking

1 Look at these film titles. They are all linked to cities. Match the films with the cities.

1 *L.A. Confidential* ——————— a) New York
2 *Bridget Jones's Diary* ———— b) Los Angeles
3 *Moulin Rouge*   c) Sheffield
4 *The Full Monty*   d) Paris
5 *All About My Mother*   e) Barcelona
6 *Breakfast at Tiffany's*   f) London

2 Check your answers with a partner. Which of the films have you seen? Which of the cities have you visited?

3 What differences are there between Los Angeles and Sheffield, do you think?

Reading & Vocabulary

1 Which of these words and phrases do you associate with:

a) Sheffield   b) Los Angeles   c) both?

> beaches b)   cheap   'city on the move'   discos   happy families
> housing estates   movie stars   orange groves   'paradise on earth'
> shops   steel   sun   top soccer teams   working man

2 The films *L.A. Confidential* and *The Full Monty* start with city descriptions. Read the descriptions below. Which words from exercise 1 are used to describe each city?

3 Find examples of the following in the texts and complete the table.

Positive language	Imperatives	Exaggeration	Slogan
happiness and prosperity		paradise on earth	heaven on America's west coast

4 Do you believe the texts? Why do they use positive language?

Sheffield

Los Angeles

L.A. Confidential

Welcome to Los Angeles – a land of beaches, sun and orange groves.
It has the best climate in the world. By day, just sit by the pool, get a perfect tan and watch life pass you by …
And, by night, watch America's most beautiful movie stars in Sunset Boulevard's bars and restaurants.
It's paradise on earth – a place where happy families walk down streets free of crime. It's a world full of colour, peace and opportunity.
That's L.A. – heaven on America's west coast.

OFF THE RECORD, ON THE QT
AND VERY HUSH-HUSH...

L.A. Confidential

"The Best Film Of Last Year"
Barry Norman, Film '98

18

THE FULL MONTY

Come to Sheffield - a city on the move! Life is cheap and there are jobs for all. This is thanks to Sheffield's number one industry, steel - the metal that generates happiness and prosperity.
Here, every working man can buy his own home in the most modern housing estates in Europe.
But that's not all. We have the best shops, two of Britain's top soccer teams and at night the most exciting discos in the north of England. You'll never want to leave!
That's Sheffield - an unforgettable experience!

12

 **Describing where places are:** Try exs 1–2 on your CD-Rom.

Writing

Sell your town

1 Write an advert for your city / town. Look at the table in Reading & Vocabulary exercise 3. Add expressions to describe where you live.

EXAMPLE: Positive language – dynamic

2 Now write the advert. Complete the gaps.

EXAMPLE: <u>Come</u> to <u>Tarragona</u>, the most <u>dynamic</u> place in <u>Catalunya</u>!

_____ (*imperative*) to _____ (*your city / town*), the most _____ (*adjective*) place in _____ ! (*country*)

There are hundreds of _____ (*noun*) to _____ (*verb*). You can visit _____ (*place*) and _____ (*place*), and then _____ (*verb*). And at night you can _____ (*verb*) until the early hours.

Life is good in _____ (*city / town*). It's _____ (*exaggeration*)! But don't forget that it's very _____ (*adjective*), so be careful that you don't _____ (*verb phrase*).

Come to _____ (*exaggeration*). _____ (*slogan*).

TAKEAWAY ENGLISH: *Giving directions*

1 Read the invitation. Complete the gaps with words from the box.

~~catch~~	come out	left	next	opposite
past	stop	straight	turn	until

> ### You're invited to a cocktail party to celebrate Martin and Clare's 5th wedding anniversary.
>
> #### We kick off at 9pm. Bring a bottle and dress cool!!
>
> From King's Cross Station, [1]*catch* a train from platform 12. (This is the fast train.) Cambridge is the last [2]_____ . [3]_____ of the station and turn [4]_____ into Station Road. Walk [5]_____ down the hill [6]_____ you get to Graves Road. [7]_____ left here, then take the [8]_____ right into Hill Street. Walk [9]_____ the Botanical Gardens and about two minutes later, turn into Londsdale Gardens. Our house is no. 19 and is [10]_____ the Queen's Head pub. You can't miss it! Or if you're feeling lazy, take a taxi!

2 (1.8) Listen to three people giving directions. Answer the questions.

1 Where does each person want to go?
2 How are they travelling?
3 Is their destination near or far?
4 Is the person giving directions helpful?

3 Listen again. What directions do you hear?

EXAMPLE: Take the first right ...

4 Work in pairs.

Student A: Turn to page 119. Student B: Turn to page 121.

Useful language	
Asking	**Answering**
How do I get to ...?	Go straight down ...
Excuse me. Do you know where ... is?	Turn right / left. Take the next right / left.

Song

(1.9) *New York, New York*: See resource sheet 1B.

BRITAIN'S FAVOURITE COMEDY
THE FULL MONTY
(15)

Now do Unit test 1 on your CD-Rom. 13

2 Lives and loves

- Past Simple & Past Continuous
- used to
- Describing people
- Relationship verbs
- /ʃ/
- Chatting up

Ideal partners

Vocabulary
Describing people

1 Look at these dialogues. Which one refers to appearance? Which one refers to personality?

1 'What's he like?' 'He's really friendly.'
2 'What does she look like?' 'She's tall.'

2 Put the adjectives into the correct category: personality (P) or appearance (A).

EXAMPLE: bald – A   easy-going – P

~~bald~~   blonde   dark   ~~easy-going~~   good-looking
grey-haired   kind   outgoing   sensible   sensitive
short   slim   sociable   tanned   trendy

Note: A **sensible** person uses a lot of common sense. A **sensitive** person feels things very intensely.

Speaking

1 Look at the photos. What do you consider attractive or beautiful?

EXAMPLE: I like tall people. I like blonde hair.

2 Which famous people do you think are attractive? Why?

3 What is more important to you: appearance or personality? Why?

Speaking & Listening

1 Look at the photos. In pairs, describe each person. What do they look like? What are they like, do you think?

EXAMPLE: 'a' has got blonde hair. She looks sporty.

2 Each person in photos a–d is linked with a person in the photos below. Who's with who? Guess their relationship.

EXAMPLE: Sophie – d. I think they're brother and sister.

3 (2.1) Listen and check your answers. Match the names below with people a–d.

Carrie   Matthew   James   Pete

4 Listen again. Match adjectives from Vocabulary exercise 2 with people a–d.

EXAMPLE: Matthew – sensible, tanned

5 Why does each partner like the other? Give one reason.

EXAMPLE: Sophie likes Matthew because she can talk to him.

Sophie

Luke

Patricia

Danny

The Real Thing: *-ish*

1 (2.2) Listen to Luke and Sophie again.

2 Look at the examples and answer the questions.

1 *He's shortish* …
   Is Pete very short or quite short?

2 *He's fortyish* now.
   What does *-ish* mean here?

3 Translate the examples above into your language.

-ish is added to adjectives to show that something is similar but not exactly the same as the adjective.

4 Complete the sentences with these words.

fiftyish   eightish   shortish
straightish   reddish

1 I knew he was embarrassed because he went a _____ colour.
2 Let's meet after work – is _____ OK with you?
3 He's older than he looks. He must be _____.
4 He's _____, with blonde hair and blue eyes.
5 He's attractive – dark, _____ hair and lovely dark eyes.

5 (2.3) Listen and check.

Pronunciation

/ʃ/

1 How do you say this word?

British /ˈbrɪtɪʃ/

2 (2.4) Listen and check. Write down the other words you hear.

EXAMPLE: sugar

3 Tick the words with the /ʃ/ sound.

EXAMPLE: sugar ✓

4 (2.5) Listen and repeat the sentences.

1 Trish is fifty but she looks fortyish.
2 I've finished washing the dishes.
3 I wish you'd stop being so childish.
4 The beach is full of rubbish.

How we met

Speaking

Discuss these questions.

1 How do people meet each other?
2 Do you know where your parents met?
3 Which places are most romantic to meet in?

Reading

1 Work in pairs.

Student A: Read Tammy's story and answer these questions.

1 How did they meet?
2 Why was it difficult to start a relationship?

Student B: Read Albert's story and answer these questions.

1 How did they meet?
2 What is Albert's only regret?

2 Tell your partner the story.

3 Now read Petra's and Ricardo's stories. Complete them with verbs in the Past Simple tense.

> decide   go   happen   have
> introduce   invite

4 Work in pairs. Match the headings (1–4) with the four texts.

1 Across a crowded room
2 Love on-line
3 Mistaken identity
4 It's never too late

CLOSE ENCOUNTERS

These days, you can find love in all kinds of places. We talked to four couples from around the world who met their partner in a memorable way.

Tammy, 28 and Brad, 31 (USA)

Tammy: 'I was very sceptical about meeting people on the internet. But one day I was surfing the net and decided to go into a chat room. It was quite boring until a guy called Brad came into the room. We chatted for a long time and then exchanged photos. It was difficult because we were both going out with someone at the time and we were living in different states, but eventually we arranged to meet. And now we're together!'

Albert, 78 and Joyce, 80 (UK)

Albert: 'I live in an old people's home and I really thought I was too old to meet anybody special. I wasn't looking for love, but I suppose I needed a friend. One day, I was reading the newspaper in the garden when Joyce came over to have a chat. We talked and talked, day after day, and we became very close. Now, we do everything together. I have one regret – that I didn't meet Joyce years ago!'

Petra: 'It ¹_____ one night at our local nightclub. I was dancing, and suddenly I ²_____ the feeling that someone was watching me. I looked around and saw a boy on the other side of the room staring at me. I ³_____ to be brave and walked over to him. Hans was very shy but we had a drink and started talking. We just clicked and we quickly became friends.'

Petra, 19 and Hans, 20 (Germany)

Simon, 42 and Ricardo, 46 (Argentina)

Ricardo: 'It was New Year's Eve and I ⁴_____ some people around to my house to celebrate. I planned a quiet party but my friends brought other friends and by twelve o'clock there were lots of people. I was making some drinks in the kitchen when I noticed this guy on his own. He didn't seem to know anybody, so I ⁵_____ over to him and ⁶_____ myself. He said, "So you're not Antonio, then?!" He was at the wrong party – he had made a mistake with the address! I asked him to stay and we got on really well ... and now we're together.'

Language focus

Past Simple and Past Continuous

Look at the example and answer the question.

*I **was watching** television when the telephone **rang**.*

watching TV

telephone rang

9 pm   10 pm   11 pm

There are two actions in this sentence. Which one is longer?

<u>Underline</u> the correct words in the rules.

We use the **Past Continuous / Past Simple** to describe actions in progress in the past.

Find an example in the text on page 16.

....

We use the **Past Continuous / Past Simple** to describe shorter, completed actions in the past.

Find an example in the text on page 16.

....

The Past Simple action often interrupts the Past Continuous.

*I **was reading** in the garden when she **came over** to have a chat.*

Find two more examples in the text on page 16.

....
....

To form the Past Continuous, we use the verb .... / .... + -ing form.

> See Reference Guide, p. 4.
> See Workbook, pp. 9–10, exs 1–4.

Practice

1 Answer the questions with a verb in the Past Continuous. What were you doing:

  1 at two o'clock last night?
     I was sleeping.
  2 last Sunday afternoon?
  3 last Saturday night?
  4 before this lesson started?

2 Guess what your partner was doing at these times. Check with your partner to see if you were right.

Vocabulary & Writing

Relationship verbs

1 The pictures show different stages of a couple's relationship. Order the pictures to make a story.

  EXAMPLE: 1 – b

2 Match a verb with each picture.

> stay friends   meet b)   get engaged   split up   fall in love
> go out together   get married   argue   fancy each other

3 Tell the story to your partner.

  EXAMPLE: They met at a party. Paula was having a drink, when she noticed Scott ...

4 Write the story using the Past Simple and Past Continuous. Use these time expressions.

> a year later   after six months   eventually
> from time to time   immediately   soon   the next day

In groups, compare your stories.

In touch

Speaking & Listening

1 Discuss these questions.

1 Who would you say is your best friend?
2 When did you meet?
3 Why are you close?
4 How often do you see each other?
5 Do you ever argue?

2 (2.6) Listen to three people talking about best friends. Answer the questions below.

		Steve	Fran	Liam
1	Name of best friend	Bill		
2	Where did they meet?			
3	Why do / did they get on well?			
4	Do / did they ever argue?			
5	Are they still in touch? If not, what is the reason?			

Now match the friends with their photos a–c.

Language focus

used to

1 (2.7) Listen and complete the sentences.

1 We always _____ _____ _____ together at school.
2 We both _____ _____ _____ in Oxford.
3 Believe it or not, my best friend _____ _____ _____ my ex-girlfriend.

Turn to Reference Guide, page 39, and check your answers in transcript 2.7.

2 Look at transcript 2.6 in your Reference Guide, page 39. Underline all the sentences with *used to*.

> **used to**
>
> Look at the examples and underline the correct word in the rule.
>
> We **used to do** everything together, but now we don't.
> We **used to play** together at school.
>
> We use *used to* to talk about habits or states in the **present / past**.
>
> | + | I **used to** work at home. |
> | – | I **didn't use** to sleep well when I was younger. |
> | ? | **Did** you **use** to play basketball? |
>
> Correct the sentences below.
>
> 1 I didn't used to go to nightclubs. ....
> 2 Did you used to go to school? ....
> 3 I use to speak French. ....
>
> > See Reference Guide, p.5.
> > See Workbook, p.10, exs 5–8.

Memorable situations: *Try exs 1–5 on your CD-Rom.*

Practice

1 Make sentences with *used to*.

1 <u>I used to smoke</u> before I had children. (I / smoke)

2 _____ when he lived in London. (he / not / drive)

3 _____ but now we get on better. (we / argue / all the time)

4 _____ before the accident? (you / do / sport)

5 _____ when you were a child? (you / play / with trains)

6 _____ but now I have one. (I / never / want a car)

2 Make sentences with *used to* about a friend, or girl/boyfriend. What has changed in your relationship?

EXAMPLE: We used to meet every week, but now it's once a month.

Speaking

1 Think about yourself now and ten years ago. What has changed? Make a list.

	Now	Ten years ago
Appearance	Have short hair	Had long hair
Town / city		
Personality		
Job		

2 Work in pairs. Ask and answer questions about how your lives have changed.

EXAMPLE: A: How has your appearance changed?
B: I used to have long hair but now it's short.

Reading & Speaking

1 Are you a true friend? Do the questionnaire on the right then turn to page 122 to find out.

2 In pairs, compare your scores. Who is a better friend? Do you agree with the results?

Are you a true friend?

1 You are at a party. Your best friend is ill because s/he has drunk too much. You ...

a) go home and leave him / her at the party – s/he knows what s/he's doing.
b) take him / her home with you.
c) pretend you don't know him / her – it's embarrassing!

2 Your best friend desperately needs some money to pay the rent. You ...

a) give him / her the money. It's a present.
b) lend him / her the money.
c) don't give him / her the money – money and friendship don't go together!

3 Your best friend has bought a dress just like yours. You ...

a) tell him / her to change it – you don't want to look like twins.
b) feel happy about it – it shows that you have similar tastes.
c) don't think about it – these things happen.

4 Your best friend tells you a really big secret. You ...

a) don't tell anyone.
b) try not to tell anyone but it's too difficult! Soon a lot of people know.
c) tell one other good friend.

5 Your new partner doesn't get on with your best friend. You ...

a) stop being friends – your new partner is more important.
b) explain to your partner that your best friend is really important to you.
c) never see both of them at the same time.

6 Your best friend is having problems with his / her partner. You ...

a) don't want to hear about it. It's your best friend's problem.
b) think your best friend is right.
c) can see both sides of the story.

Just good friends

Reading & Speaking

1 Discuss the following questions.

  1 Do you like soap operas? Why / Why not?
  2 Which are the most popular soap operas in your country?
  3 Do you have a favourite soap opera? Why do you like it?

2 Read this introduction to the American TV series *Friends*. Have you seen it?

> The comedy series *Friends* ran for a record nine seasons. It started in 1994 and it has remained the number one comedy in the United States, making its lead characters millionaires.
>
> The series focuses on the friendship of three men and three women. They meet at each other's apartments and relax at Greenwich Village's *Central Perk* coffee house.

Monica

Chandler

3 Look at the photos of the friends and match them with these jobs.

> businessman   chef   fashion executive
> out-of-work actor palaeontologist singer / songwriter

4 Guess the personality of the people in the photos. Think of an adjective to describe each one.

5 Read the text and check your answers.

6 Fill in the *Friends* relationship chart with the correct names.

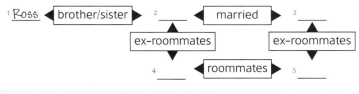

¹ Ross ◄ brother/sister ► ² ____ ◄ married ► ³ ____
ex–roommates   ex–roommates
⁴ ____ ◄ roommates ► ⁵ ____

Ross

Rachel

Monica is a chef who is obsessively tidy. She is the central figure in the series. She is now married to Chandler.

Chandler is the most sarcastic 'friend'. He works in a boring business job and has a great sense of humour.

Ross is Monica's brother. He married a lesbian, Carol, and has a son, Ben. He works as a palaeontologist in a natural history museum and is the most intelligent and romantic of the friends. He is always unlucky in love. He has an on / off relationship with Rachel.

Rachel works as a fashion executive and is quite spoilt. She has had lots of ups and downs but hasn't stopped looking for love. She used to share an apartment with Monica but now she lives with Joey.

Joey is a simple out-of-work actor. He loves sports, women, food and ... women! The other friends laugh at his macho character. He used to share an apartment with Chandler.

Phoebe is a new-age hippy singer / songwriter. She sees the good in everyone. For many viewers, she is the series' funniest and most unpredictable character. She lives alone.

Joey

Phoebe

Try the internet activities for this unit at www.webframework.net.

Writing

A soap opera

1 Write your own version of *Friends*. Choose three men and three women from the list of characters.

LOCATION: London / Sydney / San Francisco

THE BOYS	THE GIRLS

Andrew (33): A rich English lawyer. He's looking for a girlfriend.	Marta (21): A Spanish au pair just arrived in the city.

Humberto (24): A Puerto Rican model and womaniser.	Isabel (30): A single mother. She's a singer.

Claude (30): A divorced businessman with a child.	Amy (28): An American actress and sports enthusiast.

Patrick (25): A French professional football player. He's bisexual.	Cathy (32): An English businesswoman. She works in advertising.

Seb (22): An out-of-work English artist.	Tanya (27): A fashion designer and guitarist.

2 Complete the gaps to write an episode.

BACKGROUND

The programme takes place in _____. _____ lives with _____. _____ shares a flat with _____. _____ is going out with _____. _____ is _____ girlfriend.

EPISODE 24

In this episode, _____ and _____ decide to _____. _____ is angry because he / she realises that _____ is having an affair with _____. _____ and _____ go to _____ for a special _____. _____ tells _____ a secret about _____. In the end _____ finds out the secret and _____. Meanwhile _____ is particularly happy about _____. _____ and _____ have a terrible argument about _____.

The episode finishes with _____ and _____ sorting out their problems.

TAKEAWAY ENGLISH: *Chatting up*

A chat-up line shows someone that you are interested in him / her and you want to break the ice. Can you think of any chat-up lines in your language?

1 (2.8) Listen to three conversations. Where are the couples?

2 Listen again. Tick (✓) the chat-up lines you hear. Are they successful?!

a) Do you come here often?
b) Can I get you a drink?
c) Are you on your own?
d) How do you know X?
e) Has anyone ever told you you've got beautiful eyes?
f) Excuse me, have you got a light?
g) Do you know where the toilet is?
h) Your face is really familiar.

3 How good are the chat-up lines in exercise 2? Give them a score (10 = the best, 1 = the worst). Compare your answers with a partner.

4 In pairs, invent your own dialogues. Choose a place and a chat-up line – good or bad!

EXAMPLE: A: Has anyone ever told you you've got beautiful eyes?
B: Errr, no. See you!

Now do Unit test 2 on your CD-Rom.

Work it out

- Present Perfect
- *for* & *since, yet*
- Jobs
- Job adjectives
- /j/ & /dʒ/
- A job interview

A job for life?

Speaking & Vocabulary

Jobs / Job adjectives

1 Have you ever worked? What would be your ideal job? Why?

2 Match the adjectives with the jobs in the photos.

> badly-paid   boring   creative   interesting
> repetitive   skilled   sociable   stressful
> tiring   well-paid

3 In pairs, discuss your ideas.

EXAMPLE: A: Bouncers have a very sociable job.
B: I don't think it's sociable because you don't have time to talk to people.

4 Which of these jobs would you like to do? Which would you dislike? Why?

EXAMPLE: I'd hate to be a bouncer because I don't like nightclubs.

> **Useful language**
>
> I'd really like to be a ...   I wouldn't mind being a ...
> I'd love to be a ...   I'd hate to be a ...

dentist

solicitor

librarian

web designer

bouncer

gardener

teacher

lifeguard

lorry driver

artist

Jobs: Try exs 1–3 on your CD-Rom.

Listening

1 🔊(3.1) Listen to three people talking about their jobs. What do they do? How long have they done these jobs?

2 Listen again and answer the questions.

1 Who works in an office? *Sadie*
2 Who is badly-paid?
3 Who wears a uniform?
4 Who has a lot of experience?
5 Who only works at night?
6 Who has a repetitive job?

Check your answers with a partner.

3 Who is the most positive about his / her job? Who is the most negative? Why?

Tony

Sadie

Richard

Language focus
Present Perfect

> Look at the example and answer the question.
>
> SADIE: *I don't know why **I've worked** here for so long. **It's been** nearly two years.*
>
> Is she talking about a job she did in the past or one she does now?
>
> The **Present Perfect** tense describes actions that started in the past and continue into the present.
>
> We form the Present Perfect with *have / has +*
> ....
>
> Look at these sentences.
>
> *Jill's a doctor. She started working twenty years ago.*
>
>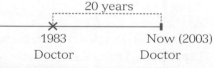
>
> Put the information into one sentence.
>
> *Jill* .... *a doctor for twenty years.*

Present Perfect and Past Simple

She worked in a shop for two years.
She has been a famous actress for over 25 years.

Which time period is **finished**? Which tense do we use? Which time period continues **up to now**? Which tense do we use?

Match the time expressions with the correct usage.

Finished time	Time up to now
....	....

two years ago   for ten years   last night
this week   yesterday   never

> *See Reference Guide, pp. 5–6.*
> *See Workbook, p.15, exs 1–3.*

Practice

Choose the correct verb form: Past Simple or Present Perfect.

1 I **had / have had** a job in a warehouse last year.
2 My sister **went / has been** for a job interview yesterday.
3 Jason has a great job in New York – he **worked / has worked** there for two years.
4 When I was a student, I **wanted / have wanted** to be an astronaut.
5 I **didn't do / haven't done** much work recently.
6 She **earned / has earned** more money than me in January.
7 I **never went / have never been** to China, but I'd love to go one day.
8 I **knew / have known** her for years.

The Real Thing: *you see / let me see*

1 🔊(3.2) Listen and complete.

RICHARD: What are the good points?! _____ – well, it gives me extra money for the summer and free time during the day. I only work at nights and at the weekends, _____.

2 Complete the rules with *you see* and *let me see*.

_____ is used when you are trying to **remember or think of** something.

_____ is used when you are trying to **explain** something.

3 Work in pairs. Answer the questions with *you see / let me see* and continue the conversations.

1 A: Which countries have you visited?
  B: _____ … I've been to …
2 A: Can you come to the party tonight?
  B: No, _____ I have to go …
3 A: When are you going on holiday?
  B: We're leaving on … _____ … on Thursday …
4 A: Did you pass the exam?
  B: No, _____ I didn't study very hard …

The best candidate

Speaking & Reading

1 Discuss these questions.

  1 Is it easy to find work where you live?

  2 Which of these factors is most important in getting a good job? Are there any other important factors?

> appearance   contacts
> personality   qualifications

2 Read the texts about Debbie and Alonso. Who do they need and why?

Debbie

Alonso

Debbie wants someone to take photos of her wedding and the party afterwards. She is looking for an experienced photographer who is friendly and sociable. She hopes to find someone who charges a reasonable price.

Alonso wants to have his twenty-first birthday party in a pub and good music is essential. He is looking for a DJ who has a large record collection. He wants people on the dance floor all night!

3 Debbie and Alonso found two candidates for each job (see right). Who do you think they chose and why?

> **Useful language**
>
> I think _____ is the best because ...
> I prefer _____ because ...
> _____ has more experience than _____
> _____ isn't suitable because ...

Photographers

File Edit View Favorites Tools Help

Back Forward Stop Refresh Home Search Favorites History Mail Print Edit Discuss

Address http://www.creativepeople.com/nathankershaw

Name: Nathan Kershaw

Age: 26

Occupation: Freelance photographer and artist

Experience: Nathan has worked as a photographer for five years. He specialises in photographing houses and interiors. He also does some weddings, parties and other ceremonies.

Qualities: Hardworking, reliable and friendly.

Special notes: Competitive prices.

See portfolio for more details at *Nathan@photoshop.uk*

File Edit View Favorites Tools Help

Back Forward Stop Refresh Home Search Favorites History Mail Print Edit Discuss

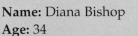

Address http://www.creativepeople.com/dianabishop

Name: Diana Bishop
Age: 34
Occupation: Professional photographer
Experience: Diana has worked as a professional photographer for ten years. Her specialist areas are major events, weddings and concerts. Last year, she photographed the Oscars for a major newspaper.
Qualities: Professional and perfectionist.
Special notes: More expensive hourly rate than some photographers.
See portfolio for more details at *Diana@photoexpress.uk*

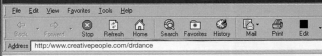

DJs

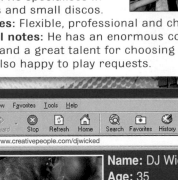

File Edit View Favorites Tools Help

Back Forward Stop Refresh Home Search Favorites History Mail Print Edit Discuss

Address http://www.creativepeople.com/drdance

Name: Dr. Dance
Age: 28
Occupation: Local London DJ
Experience: Dr. Dance has worked as a local DJ in London since he was twenty. His favourite types of music are techno, house and garage. He specialises in parties and small discos.
Qualities: Flexible, professional and cheap!
Special notes: He has an enormous collection of dance music and a great talent for choosing the perfect track. He is also happy to play requests.

File Edit View Favorites Tools Help

Back Forward Stop Refresh Home Search Favorites History Mail Print Edit Discuss

Address http://www.creativepeople.com/djwicked

Name: DJ Wicked
Age: 35
Occupation: French DJ. He has lived in London since 1990.
Experience: DJ Wicked has travelled all over the world deejaying and giving concerts. He specialises in techno and hardcore house music. He has recorded a number of DJ sessions. He is also happy to do private parties on request.
Qualities: Very experienced ... and famous!
Special notes: A real celebrity, but you have to pay for the name.

Language focus

for and *since*

Look at the examples and complete the rules with *for* or *since*.

Nathan has worked as a photographer **for** *five years.*
Dr. Dance has worked as a DJ **since** *he was twenty.*

.... is used to show the **point** at which a period of time begins.
.... is used with **periods** of time.

Find one more example of each from the texts.

....

....

How long ...?

Look at the examples and answer the questions using *for* and *since*.

How long *has Diana worked as a professional photographer?*
How long *has DJ Wicked lived in London?*

How do you say *How long* ... in your language?

> See Reference Guide, p. 6.
> See Workbook, pp. 15–16, exs 4–6.

Practice

1 (3.3) Listen and write down the words you hear.

1 six months

2 Put *for* or *since* before each phrase.

1 for six months

Listening

1 (3.4) Listen to Debbie and Alonso talking about the person they chose. Answer the questions.

1 Who did they each choose?
2 How did they make their choice?
3 Were they happy with their choice? Why / Why not?

2 (3.5) Listen again and complete the sentences.

1 She's _____ an excellent job.
2 We haven't _____ all the photos yet.
3 She's _____ us the photos of the ceremony.
4 I haven't _____ him yet.

Language focus

Present Perfect + *yet*

Look at the example.
I haven't paid DJ Wicked yet.
Has Alonso paid DJ Wicked yet?

We use *yet* in negative sentences and questions to mean 'any time up to the present'.

How do you say *yet* in your language?

> See Reference Guide, p. 6.
> See Workbook, p. 16, ex 7.

Pronunciation

/j/ *yet* and /dʒ/ *jet*

1 (3.6) Which word do you hear?

1 yet / jet 3 jaw / your 5 joke / yolk
2 yell / gel 4 job / yob 6 used / juice

2 Practice saying these words.

yacht yeah yellow yoga
yoghurt young youth yuppy

(3.7) Listen and repeat.

3 (3.8) Listen and repeat these words. How many different ways of pronouncing *y* are there?

pretty really you yoga system type reply try

4 Practise saying these sentences.

1 I don't like that type of yoghurt.
2 That's a job for yuppies.
3 I really like skiing in January.
4 Egg yolk is yellow.
5 I applied for that job but I haven't had a reply yet.

(3.9) Listen and check.

For *and* since: Try exs 1–4 on your CD-Rom. **25**

Stressed out

Speaking

Look at the photos and discuss these questions.

1 Which of the situations would you find most stressful? Why?
2 What things in your working / student life make you stressed?
3 Is stress always bad? In what ways can stress be good for you?

Reading & Listening

1 In pairs, ask and answer the questions in the stress test. If the answer is 'it depends,' say why.

2 Now work out your partner's total score from both sections.
Work
'Yes' = 0 points, 'It depends' = 5 points, 'No' = 10 points
General
'Yes' = 10 points, 'It depends' = 5 points, 'No' = 0 points

STRESS TEST

Work

Do you ...	Yes, I do	No, I don't	It depends
1 ... sleep on average less than seven hours a night?			
2 ... drink more than three cups of coffee a day?			
3 ... smoke more than ten cigarettes a day?			
4 ... often miss deadlines and hand in work late?			
5 ... arrive at work or college late more than once a week?			
6 ... work at home at the weekends and / or in the evenings?			
7 ... get angry with people at work / college for no reason?			
8 ... often feel worried about your work or studies?			
9 ... feel tired all the time?			
10 ... feel that you never have enough time?			

General

Do you ...	Yes, I do	No, I don't	It depends
1 ... do sport or exercise at least twice a week?			
2 ... go out with friends regularly?			
3 ... have a hobby or activity that you do at least once a week?			
4 ... read books for pleasure?			
5 ... have some time to relax every day?			
6 ... have a healthy diet?			
7 ... have a good circle of friends?			
8 ... talk about your feelings with family or friends?			
9 ... enjoy your job or studies?			
10 ... have regular holidays or breaks?			

3 〈3.10〉 Listen to lifestyle guru, Chad, and find out what your results mean. Do you agree with them?

4 Listen again. Match the advice with the scores.

1 150–200 points
2 100–150 points
3 50–100 points
4 0–50 points

a) Try anything – meditation, yoga, therapy …
b) Don't relax too much. Ambition isn't always a bad thing.
c) You should try to relax more in the evenings and don't let work worry you.
d) You should definitely work less, relax more and make more time for yourself.

Speaking & Reading

1 What are the alternatives to a conventional job?

2 Read the article. What jobs did these people do before and what job do they do now?

3 Answer the questions with *Fiona*, *Andy*, *Emma* or *nobody*. Who …

1 didn't have a job for a while?
   Fiona
2 has turned an interest into a profession?
3 preferred his / her old job?
4 would like to continue with their old job in some way?
5 feels he / she is doing something useful?
6 was influenced by a film that he / she saw?

4 Find words and expressions in the article related to work.
   EXAMPLE: rat race

5 Discuss the advantages and disadvantages of:

1 working at home
2 working abroad
3 doing voluntary work
4 setting up your own business

Rat race rebels

Most of us have to get on the train in the morning and go to work for a large part of every weekday. We're trapped in the rat race of material success. We interviewed three people who have said 'No!' to the nine-to-five routine. Let's meet them.

After university, I was on the dole for a few months. I didn't have any money so I was really pleased to get an office job, but it was very boring! I gave it up and went to do voluntary work for the VSO – Voluntary Service Overseas – in Rwanda. It's probably not right for everybody – you have to want to make a change in your life. I teach old people and children to read and write. I also have experience as a nurse, so I help out with basic medical aid as well. It's not exactly luxurious but it doesn't matter because it's great to do something really useful for a change.

Fiona

I used to be a freelance news journalist. It was very stressful and I had to travel a lot. I applied for lots of other jobs with no success, and I started to think about my real interests. My big obsession has always been football. So now I work from home and I write football articles for the internet and press agencies all over the world. I also run the Everton Football Club website – I'm a big fan! It's a full-time job but I have much more free time. And now I'm my own boss, I can get up when I want!

Andy

I used to be a teacher and I worked 40 hours a week – what a nightmare! Then I saw the film *American Beauty* and I thought I could change my life too! So, I discovered alternative medicine. I did a course in acupuncture and shiatsu massage. It took four years to get qualified but now I can set up my own business. I think I'd like to work from home. Shiatsu is very popular these days because people are so stressed, and you can earn quite good money. I'd like to teach part-time too if I can. It's good to do different things – if you always do the same job, it gets really boring!

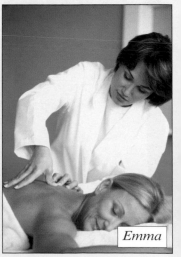
Emma

In the hot seat

Speaking & Reading

1 Have you ever had a job interview? Was the experience good or bad?

2 Here is some interview advice. Which do you think is good advice? Which is bad advice? Why?

   1 Establish eye contact with the interviewer.
   2 Ask the interviewer a lot of questions about the job.
   3 Fold your arms and cross your legs.
   4 Dress smartly. A suit is a good idea.
   5 Only speak when you are asked a question.
   6 Lie about your work experience.
   7 Talk about your good qualities even when not asked.
   8 Say why you are interested in the job.
   9 Complain about your last job.
   10 Say that you are going to other job interviews.

3 Read the adverts. In pairs, discuss the advantages and disadvantages of each job.

4 Look at the application letter and the job adverts. Answer the questions in pairs.

   1 Which job is Heather applying for?
   2 Do you think she'll get the job? Why / Why not?

GARDENER WANTED

to clean and tidy council garden areas in Manchester town centre.

- Love of nature a must
- Knowledge of plants a bonus
- Working hours: 7am – 4pm

Call Phil on: 07788-678-342

MEET THE RICH AND FAMOUS!

Wanted!

LIMOUSINE CHAUFFEUR

to drive celebrities around London.

- Smart appearance essential.
- Clean driving licence.
- Night work only.
- Salary negotiable.

Contact: juan@driversunlimited.co.uk

---

website designer

needed for young marketing company.

Have you got:

- *experience in software design?*
- *fresh ideas?*

Are you able to:

- *work nights and weekends?*

Then please e-mail us at:
vacancy@nooideas.net

(Salary according to experience.)

@ nooideas

DO **YOU** WANT TO BE A MODEL?

If you're attractive and ambitious, ***call us!***

- *Age: 17–22*
- *No experience needed*
- *Good looks essential!*

Please apply in writing to:
Model Essential,
59 Church Street Mews,
London

(Please attach a photo.)

60 Nelson's Row,
Clapham
London
SW4 0TT
Tel: 0207 777 7877

17th May, 2003

Dear Sir / Madam,

I am writing in response to your advertisement in *The Evening Standard* of 9th May.

I am 22 years old and studying computer science at the University of London. I am currently in my final year and I hope to work in Information Technology in the future.

At the moment, I'm looking for work in a different field. I have never worked as a _____ before but people tell me that I have potential. I have long, light brown hair and brown eyes (see attached photo), and I'm prepared to work hard.

I look forward to hearing from you soon.

Yours faithfully,

Heather Black

E-mail: heatherb@ucla.co.uk

Writing

A job application letter

Write a short letter applying for one of the jobs on page 28.

Useful language

I am writing to apply for the position of …

I have worked as …   I can …
I have experience as …   I am good at …ing
I am currently …

I look forward to hearing from you soon.

Listening

1 **(311)** Tom and Hannah both have an interview for one of the jobs opposite. Listen and answer the questions.

 1 Which job are the candidates applying for?
 2 What experience does each candidate have?
 3 What do they have in common?
 4 Who does a better interview – Tom or Hannah? Why? What mistakes does the other make?

2 Listen again and check your answers.

TAKEAWAY ENGLISH: *A job interview*

1 Work in pairs. You work in a recruitment agency. Your partner is looking for a job.

   Student A: Turn to page 118.
   Student B: Turn to page 120.

2 Student A: You are the interviewer.
   Student B: You are the interviewee.

   Interview your partner. Which of the three jobs suits him / her best?

3 Swap roles.

Useful language

Have you had experience of …?
Have you ever … (worked in this field)?
Are you … (computer literate)?
Can you … (work at night / long hours etc.)?
Are you interested in …?

Now do Unit test 3 on your CD-Rom.

Jobs and cities

Travis & Sarah

Michael

Julieta & Oliver

Gill

Zheng

Iqbal

Tracey

Luke

Introduction

1 Work in pairs. Test your memory. Where are these people from? Do you remember anything else about them?

2 ▮ [00:00-01:14] Watch the introduction and check your answers.

Vox pops

▮ [01:15-02:01] Watch the vox pops and answer the on-screen questions.

1 Watch again. Who says it?

1 It's a very busy place …
2 I like it because it's a big mess …
3 It is too big and it is too expensive.

2 Test your memory. Complete the gaps.

MICHAEL: If you're in a _____ mood, it's a _____ place to live. If you're in a _____ mood, it can get very _____.

LUKE: It's got lots of _____ things and lots of _____ things, but it's where I'm from.

OLIVER: I like London but it is too _____ and it is too _____.

Watch again and check your answers.

Before you watch

1 Discuss in pairs. What do you think of your city / town?

EXAMPLE: I like it because it's big and interesting …

2 Find the opposite adjectives in the box.

> stressful   boring   ~~cheap~~   noisy
> ~~expensive~~   quiet   exciting   relaxing

cheap ≠ expensive

Which of these adjectives would you use to describe your city?

While you watch

Sequence 1 [02:02-03:14]

> **prop** /prɒp/ (n): a piece of furniture or small object used in a play or a film.

Zheng works for a TV production company as a prop master. She provides the 'props' for TV programmes.

▮ Watch sequence 1 and answer the questions.

1 Where is Zheng when we first see her?

a) in the TV production company's office
b) in the prop shop
c) in the studio

2 Zheng gets the props in three ways. What are they?

3 Zheng has lived in three world cities. Put the cities in the order you see them.

a) Leeds   b) Delhi   c) Beijing

4 In which city did Zheng …

1 do a degree in Commerce?
2 do a degree in Communication Studies?
3 go to school?

🔘 *Watch programme 1 on your DVD.*

Sequence 2 [03:15-04:02]

 Watch sequence 2 and answer the questions.

1 How long has Zheng worked as a prop master?

2 What adjectives does she use to describe her job?

3 What job did she use to do?

4 Zheng talks about the cat. What kind of programme did she need it for?

5 Zheng talks about the skeleton. Tick (✓) the correct statements.

   1 It took a week to find the skeleton.
   2 The skeleton's name is Mr Freddie.
   3 The skeleton is her favourite prop.

Sequence 3 [04:03-05:04]

1 What would you expect to find in Chinatown?

2 ◼ Watch sequence 3 and check your answers. Which of these sentences is false?

   1 Zheng goes to Chinatown …
     a) when she misses China.
     b) to buy food.
     c) to eat out.
   2 Zheng thinks …
     a) the food in London is sometimes ten times more expensive than in Beijing.
     b) the food is the only thing which is more expensive in London.
     c) Beijing and London are similar in lots of ways.

3 What type of work contract has Zheng got?

   a) freelance   b) full-time   c) part-time

Sequence 4 [05:05-06:35]

1 ◼ [05:05-05:44] Watch part 1 of sequence 4 without sound. Answer the questions below.

   1 What is Zheng doing in these scenes?
   2 What do you think she needs these props for?

2 Now watch with sound. Check your answers.

3 ◼ [05:45-06:35] Now watch the rest of the sequence. Answer the questions.

   1 What will Zheng's next 'job' be?
   2 What props will she need?

Watch the whole DVD again and answer the on-screen questions.

After you watch

Can you remember?
1 What props are there in the prop shop?
2 What colours does Zheng paint the bottles?

World culture:
Hong Kong

1 Joshua Gordon lives and works in Hong Kong. We asked him some questions about his life there.

Why did you come here? To work for an English bank. I have a two-year contract.
What language do people speak here? Most people speak Cantonese, but 2% of the population speaks English. This is because Hong Kong used to be British – the handover to China was in 1997.
What do you like about the city? It's an amazing, vibrant place – a real mixture of sounds, sights and smells. It's here that 'East meets West'.
Can you explain how 'East meets West'? Well, you might find a Taoist shrine in the middle of an ultra-modern skyscraper. You can eat in local Chinese places or in European restaurants.
Is there anything you dislike about Hong Kong? Well, the divide between rich and poor is very noticeable here. Also, it's crowded and quite dirty and the humidity in the summer is unbearable.
And what about the people? The Chinese are usually friendly but they can be rude on the metro in the rush hour!
Can you tell us one last thing you especially love? The restaurants are the best in the world!
Can you tell us one last thing you hate? The cost of everything, and the obsession with mobile phones.
And any advice for visitors? Come in the spring or autumn – the summer is just too hot and humid.

2 Answer the questions.
   1 Why do some people speak English in Hong Kong?
   2 When are the people not very friendly?
   3 Why is it not a good idea to visit in the summer?
   4 Why is Hong Kong a unique city for Joshua?
   5 What positive and negative adjectives does Joshua use to describe Hong Kong?
   6 Would you like to visit Hong Kong?

Flashback 1

Vocabulary & Speaking

1 a Make eight compound nouns.

> ~~centre~~   traffic   block   store   theme
> industrial   sports   ring   road   centre
> department   tower   estate   park   jam
> ~~shopping~~

EXAMPLE: shopping centre

Look at Unit 1 to check your answers.

b In pairs, discuss where you can find these things in your town / city.

2 a Match the two parts of the sentences.

1 We had lunch together and we fell in love immediately.
2 Six months later, in June, we got …
3 I was at a conference when I met …
4 The good thing is we have stayed …
5 Things got worse and we decided to split …
6 Years later we still keep in …
7 We had busy lives and didn't start going …
8 We went skiing that Christmas and decided to get …
9 We fancied …
10 After the wedding, we were happy but soon we …

a) touch by e-mail.
b) out together until later that year.
c) married.
d) my first husband.
e) friends.
f) were arguing about everything.
g) ~~in love immediately.~~
h) each other from the start.
i) engaged on New Year's Eve.
j) up.

b In pairs, order the sentences to make a love story.

EXAMPLE: 1 I was at a conference when I met …

c Close your books. Tell each other the story from memory.

3 a Match the words below with the questions.

> ~~good-looking~~   noisy   grey-haired   kind
> crowded   badly-paid   touristy   tiring
> skilled   easy-going   sensible   trendy
> sociable   polluted   tanned

1 What's your city like?
2 What does he / she look like? good-looking
3 What are you like?
4 What's your job like?

b Look at Units 1–3 to check your answers. Find one more adjective to answer each question.

Listening

1 a (F1.1) Listen to the job interview. What job is it for?

b Complete these sentences about the interviewee.

1 He's worked in a shop before.
2 He used to _____.
3 He hasn't _____.
4 He's interested _____.
5 He can _____.
6 He's available _____.

c Listen again and write the interviewer's questions.

EXAMPLE: Have you worked in a shop before?

Language focus

1 Write questions about the film *American Beauty*. Use the poster to help you find the answers.

  1 When / film / come out?
    When did the film come out? January 2000.
  2 How many Oscars / win?
  3 Who / direct / film?
  4 Who / play / leading role?
  5 What role / Annette Bening / play?
  6 Who / Lester / fall in love with?
  7 What / be / film about?
  8 Who / write / screenplay?

2 a Complete the descriptions of famous film scenes with the verbs in the Past Simple or Past Continuous.

Gone with the Wind

1 Scarlett took Ashley into a room. When he
¹_____(ask) her what she ²_____(do), she told him she loved him. Ashley told her he ³_____(not have) the same feelings. Scarlett ⁴_____(not know) that

in a dark corner of the room Rhett ⁵_____(listen) to the conversation. Ashley left and Scarlett threw a vase at the wall in frustration. Rhett got up and asked, 'Has the war started?'

Casablanca

2 Rick ¹_____(play) cards in his bar when pianist Sam ²_____ (start) playing the song *As Time Goes By*. Rick ³_____(get up) angrily to ask Sam why he ⁴_____(play) the song. Suddenly Rick saw

why. His ex-lover Ilsa ⁵_____(stand) next to the piano. Rick and Ilsa looked at each other in silence until Inspector Renault and Ilsa's husband came up to them.

  b Write a description of a famous meeting in a film. Read your description to the class. Can other students guess the film and the actors?

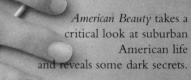

AMERICAN BEAUTY
...look closer

Released: January 2000

Winner of 5 Oscars

Best picture ★ Best director ★ Best actor ★ Best screenplay ★ Best photography

42-year-old Lester Burnham (Kevin Spacey) is having a mid-life crisis. He feels bored and frustrated at work. At home his wife (Annette Bening) and his teenage daughter (Thora Birch) don't talk to him. But everything changes when Lester falls in love with his daughter's school friend Angela (Mena Suvari). He remembers that life didn't use to be so dull...

American Beauty takes a critical look at suburban American life and reveals some dark secrets.

Starring
18 **Kevin Spacey Annette Bening Thora Birch**
Director: Sam Mendes
Screenplay: Alan Ball

You *choose!*

1 a Work in pairs. Think of an unusual job. Write questions for an interview for the job. Interview other students, but don't say what the job is.

  b Discuss the candidates and choose the best person for the job. Can the interviewees guess what the job is?

  OR

2 Write a review of a book or film. Compile a class magazine of book and film reviews.

  OR

3 Write a love story based on the photos below. Describe the following:

- Appearance and personality
- How and when they met
- What happened in their relationship

Include vocabulary and structures from Units 1–3.

- Modal verbs 1
- Modal verbs 2
- Sports equipment and places
- Attributes for sport
- /n/ & /ɴ/
- Joining a gym

On the ball

Speaking

Discuss these questions.

1 Which is your favourite sport? Why do you like it?
2 Do you play it, watch it or both?
3 What sports do you dislike? Why?
4 Which sports do you associate more with men or women? Why?

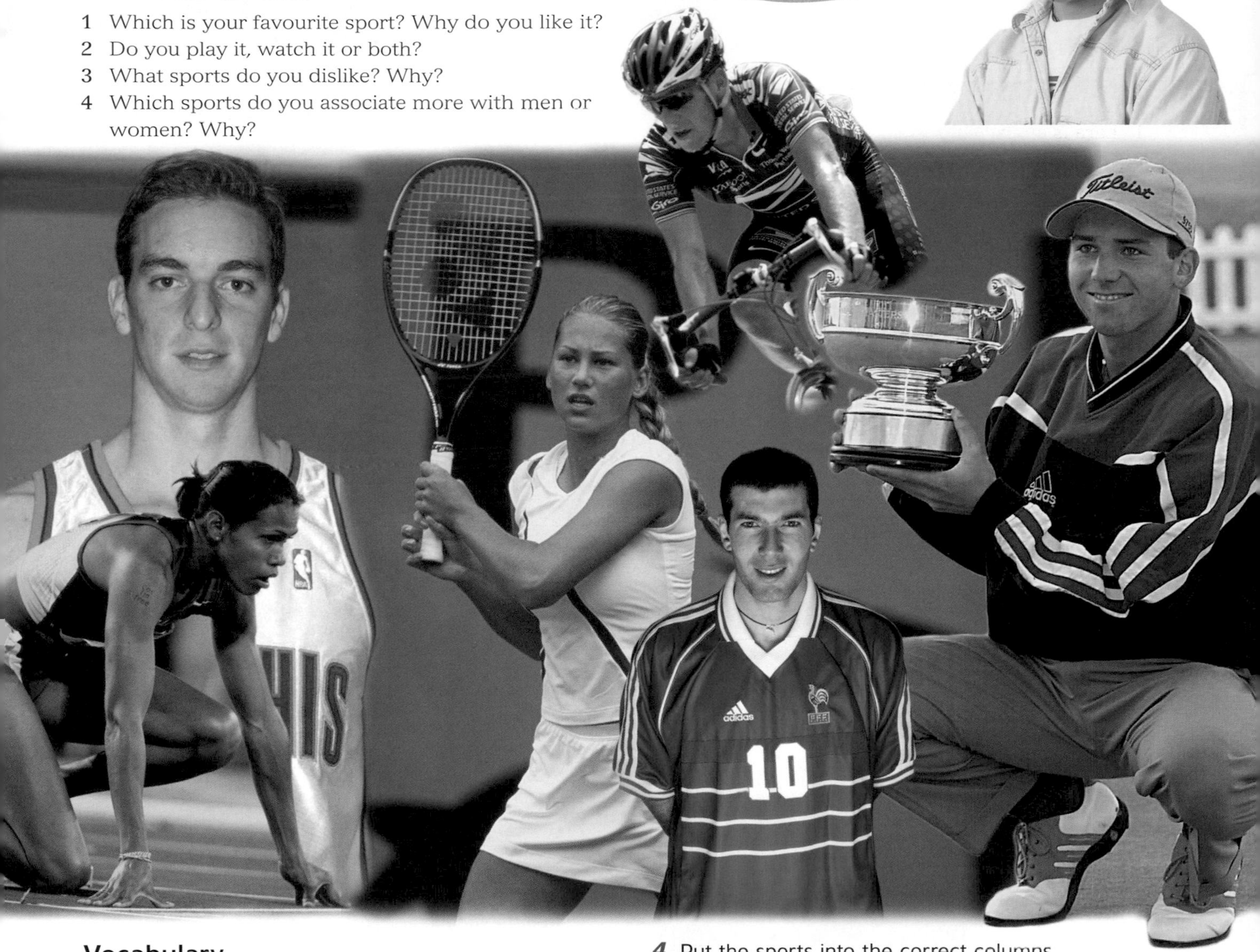

> My favourite sport is squash. I love it because it's really fast – afterwards you feel great!

Vocabulary

Sports

1 Look at the sports people above. Who are they? Match them with their sports.

1 athletics *Cathy Freeman*   4 football
2 basketball   5 golf
3 cycling   6 tennis

2 In pairs, make a list of other sports.

3 Which sports can you play on your own, which in a team and which against a single opponent?

4 Put the sports into the correct columns.

play	go	do	go for a
basketball	cycling	aerobics	bike ride

~~aerobics~~   athletics   ~~basketball~~   ~~bike ride~~
chess   ~~cycling~~   football   golf   jog
running   skiing   swim   swimming
tennis   windsurfing   yoga

Note: *Go for a* is used in other common expressions, e.g. *go for a drink / walk / drive*.

Sports & sports equipment: Try exs 1–2 on your CD-Rom.

Listening

1 (4.1) Listen to five people talking about their favourite sports and complete the table. Choose from these sports. (You will not need two of them.)

> football   gym   hockey   jogging
> skiing   ~~swimming~~   yoga

	What sport do they do?	How often do they do it?	Do they enjoy it?
Lara	swimming		
Craig		not very often	
Jess			
Alex			
Melissa			

2 Listen again and answer true (T) or false (F). If false, explain why.

1 Lara is an excellent swimmer.
2 There is something Craig doesn't like about skiing.
3 Jess plays in a professional league.
4 Alex feels good when he has finished jogging.
5 Melissa says yoga is a sport like any other.

The Real Thing: *so, such*

1 (4.2) Listen and complete the sentences.

1 LARA: It's _____ _____ _____ to be in the water.
2 CRAIG: But now I can do it really well and it's
   _____ _____ _____.
3 CRAIG: And it's _____ _____ to have the snow all around you.
4 JESS: It's _____ _____ _____, and it's a great feeling when you score a goal.
5 ALEX: When I finish I'm so relaxed. It's _____
   _____ _____ _____.
6 MELISSA: I like it because it's _____ _____ _____.
7 MELISSA: It's _____ _____ _____ _____ to do.

2 Look at the examples and underline the correct words in the rules.

It's so nice.   It's such fun.

We use *so* before **an adjective / a noun**.
We use *such* before **an adjective / a noun**.

(4.3) Listen to the examples and mark the stress. How would you say them in your language?

3 In pairs, talk about the sports in Listening exercise 1. Try to use *so* and *such*.

A: I love jogging. It's just so relaxing.
B: Really? I think it's such a boring sport. I prefer hockey.

Lara

Craig

Alex

Jess

Melissa

Pronunciation

/n/ *win* and /ŋ/ *wing*

1 (4.4) Which word do you hear?

1 sin / sing
2 ran / rang
3 win / wing
4 ban / bang
5 ton / tongue
6 sun / sung

The letters *ng* at the end of a word are always pronounced /ŋ/.

2 How do you say these sports?

cycling   jogging   skiing
swimming   trekking

(4.5) Listen and check. Practise saying the words.

3 (4.6) Sometimes we add a /g/ sound when the letters *ng* are followed by another syllable. Listen and underline the words that have a /g/ sound.

anger   angle   bringing   finger
hanging   language   longest
ringing   singer   younger

Practise saying the words.

Just do it!

Speaking & Reading

1 Discuss these questions.

1 Which clothes brands / labels do you like? Why?
2 Which do you never buy? Why not?
3 Have you got any Nike or Umbro clothes? If so, what sort?

2 Work in pairs.
Student A: Read the text about Nike.
Student B: Read the text about Umbro.
Then ask your partner these questions.

1 Who founded the company?
2 When and where did the company start business?
3 What is the name of the logo?
4 Which stars have worn it?

NIKE

The history

Nike started business in the sixties when its founders Phil Knight and Bill Bowerman met at the University of Oregon. In the mid-eighties, their success grew when famous sportsmen such as basketball king Michael Jordan wore Nike gear. In 1987, they launched the Nike Air range and a year later the famous 'Just do it' slogan. Nike now sell more sports clothes and equipment than any other company.

The logo

The Nike logo is called the 'Swoosh'. Caroline Davidson created it in 1971. It represents the wing of Nike (pronounced Ni-key), the Ancient Greek goddess of victory. She earned only $35 for her design. The first shoe with this logo came out in 1972 and now it is everywhere.

The stars

Other famous sportsmen who have worn the Nike logo include the Brazilian footballer Ronaldo, the American golfer Tiger Woods and the tennis player Pete Sampras.

UMBRO

The history

Harold C. Humphreys left school at the age of 13, and in 1920 started a small workshop in Wilmslow, in the north-east of England. Over the years this little enterprise expanded, and in 1924 Umbro (Humphreys Brothers) was founded. Since then, Umbro has had links with some of the world's greatest football clubs, teams and players. In the 1966 World Cup, 15 out of the 16 teams, including the winners, England, wore Umbro shirts. The company now makes football and casual shirts, tracksuits and other football accessories.

The logo

The famous 'double diamond' logo has not changed in half a century. Indeed, between 1954 and 1994 Brazil won four World Cups wearing this famous design.

The stars

Nowadays, the most well-known stars who wear Umbro are David Beckham and Michael Owen, along with other members of England's national football squad. Umbro currently make the football shirts for more than 30 national football teams.

Vocabulary

Sports equipment and places

1 Match the words (1–10) with the clothes and equipment in the photos (a–j).

1	boots d	6	shorts
2	cap	7	socks
3	leggings	8	tracksuit
4	goggles	9	trainers / sneakers
5	racket	10	trunks

2 Match the sports (1–5) with the places where they are played (a–e).

1	athletics	a)	court
2	football	b)	course
3	golf	c)	pitch
4	swimming	d)	pool
5	tennis	e)	track

Vocabulary

Attributes for sport

1 Complete the sentences with these qualities.

> calm   concentration   muscular
> patient   ~~quick reflexes~~   stamina

1 If a little girl runs in front of your car, you have to have <u>quick reflexes</u> to avoid hitting her.

2 I can't believe he kept going for 24 hours. He's got more _____ than the rest of us.

3 If you are in an accident, stay _____ and try not to panic.

4 I hate exams. My _____ goes after an hour so I don't work well after that.

5 If you miss the 10 o'clock bus, be _____ – there are buses every 20 minutes.

6 He does weight training every day so he's very strong and _____.

Note: *be* + adjective:
> You have to **be** calm.

have + noun:
> You have to **have** stamina.

2 What sports are represented in the pictures a–h above. Which attributes are important for playing them?

EXAMPLE: Basketball players have to be tall and have quick reflexes.

Listening

(a)   (b)   (c)   (d)   (e)   (f)   (g)   (h)

1 (4.7) Listen and match the descriptions (1–8) with the pictures (a–h). Did you guess the right sports?

EXAMPLE: 1 – b

2 Listen again. Which attribute is mentioned for each sport?

EXAMPLE: 1 – fast

Language focus

Modal verbs 1

> Write the modal verbs *can*, *can't*, *have to* and *don't have to* next to their meanings.
>
> 1 It is possible. ..<u>can</u>..   3 It is not possible. ....
>
> 2 It is necessary. ....   4 It is not necessary. ....
>
> *See Reference Guide, pp. 6–7. See Workbook, p. 24, exs 1–3.*

Practice

Complete the sentences with *have to*, *don't have to*, *can* or *can't*.

1 SKIING: You <u>have to</u> have strong legs, otherwise you _____ do it for long.

2 FOOTBALL: You _____ play in the street or the park.

3 SQUASH: You _____ have quick reflexes to hit the ball.

4 CHESS: You _____ do this anywhere, but most people play at home.

5 GOLF: You _____ hit the ball well when you're stressed.

6 CYCLING: You _____ cycle up the hills. You can get off and push.

7 MARATHON RUNNING: You _____ have great stamina.

8 BASKETBALL: You _____ be tall to play this sport, but it helps.

Heroes

Reading & Speaking

1 Who is he?

He was born in 1982.
He has size 54 feet.
He is the David Beckham of Australia.

2 Work in pairs. Look at the pictures and guess what relationship they have with the person described.

Read the text. How many did you guess correctly?

3 Match the headings (a–f) with the paragraphs (1–6).

a) His life outside the pool 5
b) A lucky escape
c) His background
d) His fame
e) His sporting achievement
f) His physique

4 Test your partner's memory. Look at the pictures and ask six questions.

EXAMPLE: What size feet does he have?

5 Who are the sporting heroes in your country? Why are they are so famous?

THORPEDO!

1

Ian Thorpe was born in Paddington, Australia on 13th October 1982. His father, Ken, always wanted him to be a cricketer. But when Ian overcame a childhood allergy to chlorine, his only dream was to join his sister Christine in the pool.

2

It's easy to see why. His 1.95 metres, 96 kilos and size 54 feet give him an awesome presence in the water. It was his feet which brought him his first nickname, 'Flipper'. He swims so fast that he seems to fly through the water. So how did it all start?

Language focus
Past Simple

Look at the text and underline verbs in the Past Simple. Which verbs are irregular?

See Workbook, p. 25, ex. 6.

Listening

(4.8) Listen to two advertising executives discussing a possible candidate for a TV advert. Answer the questions.

1 What is the advert for?
2 What will the sportsperson have to do in the advert?
3 What does the man want at first?
4 Why does the woman disagree?
5 What sportsperson do they decide on in the end? Why?

3
Thorpe made his first appearance in international competition at the age of 14. His greatest feat came only three years later when he won three gold medals at the 2000 Sydney Olympic Games. He now holds world records in 200, 400 and 800 metres freestyle.

4
Australia is a nation of water babies. 85% of its population live within 30 miles of the beach and its swimmers enjoy a pin-up status similar to footballers like David Beckham in the UK. In fact, Thorpe is now Australia's number 1 national hero. There were even special Australian stamps to celebrate his Olympic victories.

5
But in spite of this superstar status, Ian has a friendly relationship with the media. He is happy to discuss his love of philosophy, grunge music, Japanese food, computer games and Calvin Klein clothes. Thorpe is also a sporting idol in the US. He even appeared once in his favourite TV show *Friends*, as well as posing as a fashion model in New York.

6
Talking of New York, Thorpe had a lucky escape from the Twin Towers attack in September 2001. He was at the World Trade Centre, but went back to his hotel room to pick up his camera. He was on his way back again when the first plane collided into the north tower.

Language focus
Modal verbs 2

(4.9) Listen again and complete the sentences.

1 It <u>has to</u> be someone with a good body.
2 It _____ be anyone famous, just someone attractive.
3 No, it _____ be someone famous. We _____ have someone unknown.
4 We _____ do more than a minute – we don't have the budget for more than that

Match the modal verbs (1–5) with their meanings (a–d). Two of the modal verbs have the same meaning.

1 can   a) you are obliged to
2 can't   b) you are not allowed to
3 have / has to   c) you are able to
4 don't / doesn't have to   d) you are not obliged to
5 mustn't

mustn't and *don't have to*

You **mustn't** touch the ball in football.
= It is prohibited or not allowed.

You **don't have to** wear a helmet to go cycling.
= It is not necessary. There is no obligation.

See Reference Guide, p. 7. See Workbook, p. 25, exs 4–5.

Practice

Complete the sentences with *mustn't, have to* or *don't have to*.

1 In golf, you <u>mustn't</u> hit the ball twice.
2 In boxing, you _____ wear special gloves.
3 Sprinters _____ run a long distance.
4 In speed skiing, you _____ turn – you can ski straight downhill.
5 In tennis, you _____ let the ball bounce more than once.
6 To be a successful sportsperson, you _____ train every day.

Pronunciation
Connected speech

1 (4.10) Listen and complete the dialogues.

1 A: You <u>mustn't</u> do it, do you understand?
   B: OK, but you _____ shout about it.
2 A: I _____ stand that new teacher.
   B: I know you _____, but what _____ we do?
3 A: I _____ work really hard next week.
   B: You _____. I'll give you a hand if you want.
4 A: I _____ swim faster than you.
   B: I don't think you _____. Just watch me!

2 Listen again and mark the modal verbs that are stressed. How do we pronounce these words when they are not stressed?

1 mustn't   a) /məsənt/   b) /mʌsənt/
2 have to   a) /hæv tu/   b) /hæf tə/
3 can   a) /kæn/   b) /kən/
4 can't   a) /kɑnt/   b) /kɜnt/

3 Practise the dialogues in exercise 1.

Is it sport?

Speaking

Look at the pictures and discuss these questions.

1. Are these sports?
2. Why are people interested in doing / watching them?
3. Do you think any of these sports should be banned? Why / Why not?

Try the internet activities for this unit at www.webframework.net.

Writing

Expressing your opinions

1 Read the composition and complete it with these linking words and expressions.

> Also,   Firstly,   Finally,   in fact,
> ~~It seems to me that~~   What is more,

BULLFIGHTING IS A TRADITION WE
SHOULD MAINTAIN

A lot of foreigners criticise Spain for
keeping the tradition of bullfighting. For
them, it is a cruel blood sport and a
grotesque spectacle. But is it really so
simple? ¹It seems to me that the question
is more complicated.

² _____ I think people go to bullfights
not only to see blood but also for the
whole spectacle – the colours, the
music, the atmosphere. ³ _____
bullfights are popular because the public
love to see the skill of the 'toreros'.

⁴ _____ the bulls do not suffer very
much. They have a very happy life before
going into the bull ring – ⁵ _____ their
owners give them very special treatment.
Perhaps all blood sports are a little
cruel, but bullfighting is no worse than
other 'sports' such as boxing or
fox-hunting.

⁶ _____ I believe that we should keep
the bullfight because it is part of
Spain's cultural identity. Can you
imagine England without cricket or
America without baseball?

---

2 Write a reply to the composition above
or write a similar composition about
another controversial sport (e.g. fox-
hunting, boxing).

Write three paragraphs.

Paragraph 1: Introduction
Paragraph 2: Reasons for and against
　　　　　　　 – put the most important
　　　　　　　 reasons first
Paragraph 3: Conclusion

TAKEAWAY ENGLISH: *Joining a gym*

1 What do you need to know before joining a gym? In pairs,
write a list.

2 Complete the conversation. Choose from these verbs.

> can   has to   have to   mustn't

CUSTOMER: Hello, I'd like to join the gym. What do I
¹have to do to become a member?
RECEPTIONIST: Well, first you ² _____ fill in this form with
your name, address and bank details. The prices are all
there on the form.
CUSTOMER: And what does membership include?
RECEPTIONIST: You ³ _____ use the swimming pool, gym
and squash courts, and there are aerobics classes too.
But you ⁴ _____ arrive late for those – the teacher won't
let you in if you're late!
CUSTOMER: OK. ⁵ _____ I come any day of the week?
RECEPTIONIST: Yes. We're open every day.
CUSTOMER: And ⁶ _____ I bring a friend with me?
RECEPTIONIST: Yes, but your friend ⁷ _____ buy a one-day
ticket.
CUSTOMER: That's fine. So when ⁸ _____ I start?
RECEPTIONIST: Right now, if you like. If you fill in the form,
I'll give you a temporary card. One more thing – you
⁹ _____ wear those trainers in the gym – they ¹⁰ _____
be clean!
CUSTOMER: Oh, all right ... thanks for you help.

(4.11) Now listen and check.

3 Match the two halves of the questions.

1 Do I have to wear　　a) a fitness programme?
2 Can I bring　　　　　b) the sauna and jacuzzi for free?
3 Can I start　　　　　c) immediately?
4 Do I have to follow　d) a cap in the pool?
5 Can I use　　　　　　e) a friend with me?

4 In pairs, act out a dialogue.

Student A: You want to join a gym and you need
information about timetable, facilities and prices.
Prepare some questions and act out the dialogue.

Student B: You work at the reception of the gym. Write
down basic information (facilities, opening times, prices,
etc.) and act out the dialogue.

 Joining a sports centre: Try exs 1–3 on your CD-Rom. Now do Unit test 4 on your CD-Rom.　**41**

5 In transit

- *will & going to*   - Holiday items   - /ɪ/
- *might*   - Travel collocations   - Booking a hotel

Ready to go

Speaking

1 Look at the photos. Which would you choose as your next holiday? Why?

I'd choose the sightseeing holiday / the cruise because …
I'd like / prefer to go camping because …

2 In pairs, discuss these questions.

1 Do you travel light?
2 What do you take with you when you go on holiday?
3 What could you not survive without?

Vocabulary

Holiday items

1 Match the words (1–14) with the pictures (a–n).

1	binoculars j	8	penknife
2	boots	9	magazine
3	camera	10	phrase book
4	compass	11	rucksack
5	first aid kit	12	sleeping bag
6	flip-flops	13	suntan cream
7	guide book	14	traveller's cheques

2 Which would you take on the holidays in the photos? Would any be useful on all three holidays?

sightseeing holiday

camping holiday

cruise

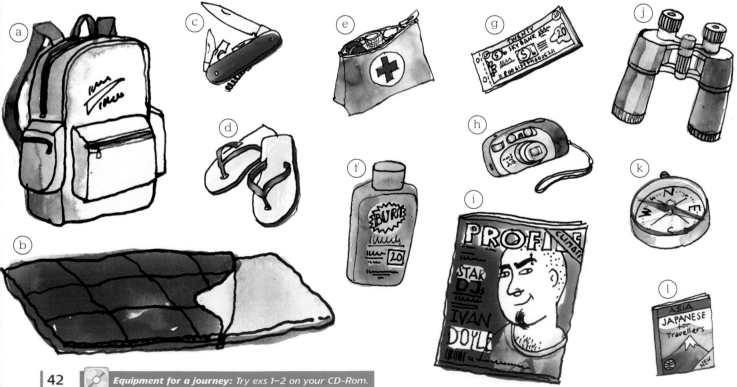

Equipment for a journey: Try exs 1–2 on your CD-Rom.

Listening

1 (5.1) Listen to three people preparing to go on holiday. Match the conversations with the holidays in the photos.

2 Listen again and complete the table.

	What should they take?	What time of year will it be?	What will the weather be like?
1	rucksack, ...		
2			cold
3			

Language focus

will

> Look at the examples and complete the rules.
>
> 1 *The nights will be cold.*
> 2 *Will it be easy to find a hotel?*
> 3 *You won't need much.*
> 4 *I'll take a notebook to write my novel.*
>
> We sometimes use .... + infinitive to talk about the future.
> We form questions with: *Will* + subject + ...…?
> The negative form of *will* is ....
> The contracted form of *will* is ....
>
> We use *will* for predictions and spontaneous decisions.
>
> ### Predictions
>
> *You'll need a really good rucksack.*
> *The nights will be cold.*
>
> Look at transcript 5.1 in your Reference Guide, page 45. Find two more predictions with *will*.
>
> ....
> ....
>
> ### Spontaneous decisions
>
> *Of course, vaccinations ... I'll do those tomorrow.*
> *A phrase book? I think my brother's got one. I'll borrow his.*
>
> Which of examples 1–4 above is a spontaneous decision? ....
>
> We often use *will* when we order food and drink.
>
> *I'll have fish and chips, please.*
>
> > See Reference Guide, p. 8.
> > See Workbook, p. 30, exs 1–2.

(m)

(n)

Practice

1 Are these sentences predictions (P) or decisions (D)?

1 It'll rain tomorrow. P
2 I'll have a white coffee and toast.
3 You won't find a ticket for the match.
4 I'll phone her now.
5 She'll love the campsite.

2 An American family is going to spend their summer holiday in your town / city. Are these sentences true (T) or false (F)?

1 It'll be really hot.
2 They won't find a hotel easily.
3 The town / city will be very crowded.
4 They'll spend a lot of time at the swimming pool.

Write six more predictions about your town to send to the family.

Pronunciation

Contractions with *will*

1 (5.2) Listen and complete the sentences.

1 __It'll__ be really cold in winter.
2 _____ be lots of places to visit.
3 _____ need a good map to get around.
4 _____ tell you where you need to go.
5 _____ lend you his camera.
6 _____ be useful.

Listen again and check. Practise saying the sentences.

2 (5.3) Listen to four conversations. In which ones is *I'll* pronounced correctly?

3 (5.4) Listen and repeat. Practise saying the sentences.

1 I'll just go and check.   4 I'll give you a hand.
2 I'll take it, thanks.   5 I'll tell you later.
3 I'll see what I can do.

How would you say these sentences in your language?

/l/

4 How do you say these words ending in /l/?

miracle   natural   table   title   travel

(5.5) Listen and check. Practise saying the words.

Speaking

1 You're planning a surprise trip to go on with your partner. Think of a destination.

2 Work in pairs. Ask your partner questions about the destination he / she has chosen for you.

EXAMPLE: What will the weather be like?
What will I need to take?
What will I be able to do?
Will it be easy to ...?

Can you guess where you are going?

City breaks

Speaking

Answer the questions.

1 What is the difference between these holidays?

> day trip   guided tour
> package holiday   weekend break

2 How often do you go on holiday or for weekends away? How long do you go for?

3 What's your favourite holiday destination?

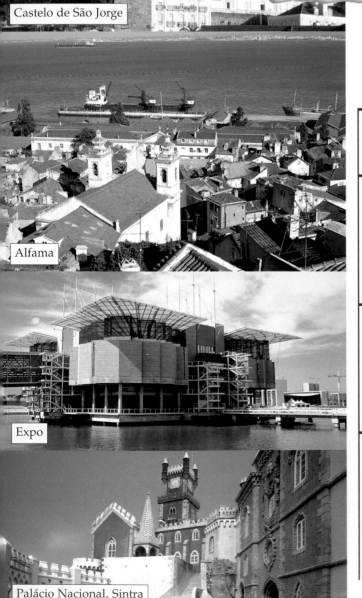

City Breaks

Castelo de São Jorge

Alfama

Expo

Palácio Nacional, Sintra

Vocabulary
Travel collocations

1 What verb do we usually use with the holidays in Speaking exercise 1?

2 Match the verbs (1–7) with the nouns (a–g).

1	book	a)	a guide book
2	buy	b)	a hotel room
3	go	c)	the sights
4	go on	d)	sightseeing
5	pack	e)	souvenirs
6	read	f)	your suitcase
7	see	g)	a trip

Note: *Travel* is usually used as a verb, e.g. *I travel a lot for my work.* We say *go on a trip* not ~~go on a travel.~~

Speaking & Reading

1 When you visit a new city, do you like to:

1 see all the sights or just a few?

2 follow a guide book or follow your nose?

3 go on a guided tour or discover the city on your own?

2 Have you ever been to Lisbon? Do you know anything about the city?

3 Read the travel itinerary. Is it a relaxed or a busy schedule?

A WEEKEND IN LISBON WITH SUNSHINE TOURS

THURSDAY
A Sunshine Tours rep will meet you at Lisbon airport and a coach will take you to your hotel.

FRIDAY
In the morning, we will take one of the city's famous yellow trams up to the Castelo de São Jorge, with fabulous views over the city. The afternoon is free for you to explore the Baixa district with its interesting shops and cafés. In the evening, we will go to the Bairro Alto area to wine and dine and hear the wonderfully melancholy *fado* music.

SATURDAY
A day of contrasts. In the morning, a trip to the oldest neighbourhood, Alfama. Its little cobbled streets are charming but it is also one of the poorest parts of the city. We will have lunch in the central Praça do Comércio and then take another tram to the new-look Lisbon – the site of the Expo, which has some stunning architecture. In the evening, you are free to enjoy whatever part of the city you wish.

SUNDAY
A coach will take us out of the city to visit Sintra, summer residence of the kings of Portugal. Here, we will see the breathtaking Palácio Nacional and walk around Sintra's beautiful woods and parks. On our way back, we will stop at Cascais, just an hour from the capital. This is a real Portuguese beach resort, full of local people and crammed with restaurants, beach cafés and discos. After a relaxing dinner on the beach, the coach will take us back to the hotel. Our return flight leaves early on Monday morning.

4 Are these sentences true (T) or false (F)? If false, explain why.

1 There is nothing organised on the Friday afternoon.
2 *Fado* music is very happy.
3 On Saturday afternoon, you will visit an old part of the city.
4 Cascais is popular with Portuguese people.
5 You will spend the whole of Sunday evening outside Lisbon.

5 Find words or expressions in the text that mean the same as the words below.

1 tour guide (Thursday) 4 wonderful (Saturday)
2 have dinner (Friday)   5 impressive (Sunday)
3 delightful (Saturday) 6 packed (Sunday)

6 *fabulous* and *stunning* are positive adjectives. How many others can you find? Why are there so many in this text?

Speaking & Listening

1 What things can go wrong on holiday?

2 Mr and Mrs Smith go on the trip to Lisbon. Predict which of these things will be a problem for them.

> beach   crowds   entertainment   flight   noise
> food and drink   hotel room   hotel staff   nightlife
> queues   shops   sights   transport   weather

3 (5.6) Listen to Mr and Mrs Smith describing their trip. Tick (✓) the things in exercise 2 that were a problem for them.

4 Listen again and complete the table with their exact problems.

THURSDAY NIGHT

Delays at airport – flight late. Arrived at hotel 3 am ...

FRIDAY

SATURDAY

SUNDAY

The Real Thing: *So do I / Nor do I*

1 Look at the examples and answer the questions.

MRS SMITH: *I really needed a holiday.*
MR SMITH: *So did I.*
MRS SMITH: *I don't like fado at all.*
MR SMITH: *Nor do I.*

1 Does Mr Smith agree or disagree with his wife?
2 How do you say *So did I* and *Nor do I* in your language?

2 (5.7) Listen and complete the conversations.

1 A: I hate package holidays.
  B: So do I.
  A: You just don't have any freedom to do what you want.

2 A: I didn't like the food in the hotel.
  B: _____
  A: It was really disgusting, wasn't it?

3 A: I don't like travelling by plane.
  B: _____
  A: It's really scary, isn't it? Especially the take-off and landing.

4 A: I went on holiday in July.
  B: _____
  A: Really? Where did you go?

Listen again and mark the stress. Practise saying the responses.

3 Look at the conversations in exercise 2 and complete the rules.

If the first sentence is positive, we start the response with _____.

If the first sentence is _____, we start the response with *Nor*.

If the first sentence is in the _____, we respond with the auxiliary verb *do*.

If the first sentence is in the Past Simple, we respond with the auxiliary verb _____.

4 Work in pairs. Imagine these sentences are true for you. Agree with them and then give more information.

EXAMPLE: I like travelling on my own.
       So do I. You can do exactly what you want.

1 I travel a lot for my work.
2 I went to the beach last summer.
3 I don't enjoy camping.
4 I have two holidays every year.
5 I didn't go on holiday last year.

Gap year

Speaking & Reading

1 Discuss these questions.

1 What is a gap year?
2 How long does it last?
3 When and why do people take one?

2 Read the text and check your answers.

15 MONTHS THAT CAN CHANGE YOUR LIFE

Teachers and students agree – a gap year is a unique experience that can change your life forever. Gap years usually begin when a student leaves school in June and last until they start higher education in October of the following year. Prince William's decision to have a gap year in Patagonia was typical of young people in the UK – they take a break from studying and see some of the world before going on to university or college. It's an opportunity to enjoy a bit of adventure, travel, maybe gain some work experience or spend some time helping other people.

3 Discuss these questions.

1 Have you ever taken a gap year?
2 Where did you go?
3 Where would you like to go if you could spend a gap year anywhere in the world?

Listening

Sarah   Adam   Raff   Karen

1 (5.8) Listen to four people talking about their plans for a gap year. Match the speakers with the photos (a–d).

2 Listen again and complete the table.

	Where are they going?	Why have they chosen this place?	What are they going to do there?	What are they going to study?
Sarah				
Adam		Wants to help people in the developing world		
Raff				Nothing
Karen				

3 In your opinion, whose gap year is going to be the most:

1 adventurous   2 relaxing   3 boring   4 interesting?

Give reasons for your answers.

Language focus

will and going to

Look at the example and complete the rules.

I'm going to try Rome first, because I think there'll be more job opportunities there.

We use _____ + infinitive to talk about plans.
We use _____ + infinitive to make predictions.

Turn to Reference Guide, page 46. Look at transcript 5.8 and find other examples of plans and predictions. Write some here.

Plans	Predictions
....	....
....	....

Remember!
We also use *will* + infinitive for spontaneous decisions.

Match the sentences (1–3) with the uses (a–c).

a) plan   b) prediction   c) spontaneous decision

1 *I'm tired. I think I'll go to bed.*
2 *I'm going to study abroad next year.*
3 *My parents will be lonely without me.*

Translate these sentences into your language.

1 ....
2 ....
3 ....

Note: For plans that are sure to happen, we use the Present Continuous, not *going to*.
I'm flying to Rio de Janeiro tonight. Look – here's the plane ticket!

> *See Reference Guide, pp. 8–9.*
> *See Workbook, pp. 30–31, exs 3–4.*

Practice

1 Are these sentences plans, predictions or spontaneous decisions? Complete them with *will* or *going to* + verb.

> carry   ~~miss~~   study   take   wear   win

1 Hurry up or you'll miss the plane.
2 Next year, I _____ Japanese in Tokyo.
3 That suitcase looks heavy. Give it to me and I _____ it for you.
4 It's very sad, but Arsenal _____ (not) the league.
5 What _____ (you) at the wedding?
6 'Oh no, look at the time!' 'Don't worry, Jim_____ you to the station.'

2 Write five sentences about your plans for next year.

EXAMPLE: *I'm going to look for a new job.*
I'm going to buy my own flat.

Read your partner's sentences. Who has the most adventurous plans?

Listening

1 Are you indecisive? Do you find it difficult to make a decision?

2 (5.9) Listen to three conversations. What is each about? Do the speakers make a decision? If so, what is it?

Language focus

might

I might stay in, or I might go to the cinema. I might not go to the party.

Read the examples above and underline the correct word in the rule.

We use *might (not)* + infinitive when something in the future is **certain / possible**.

In conversation, we often say *I might do* and *I might not* as an answer to a question.

A: *Are you going to buy a new watch?*
B: *I might do.*

A: *Are you going to buy your own flat soon?*
B: *I might not. I quite like living with my parents.*

How do you say *I might do* and *I might not* in your language?

....

> *See Reference Guide, p. 9.*
> *See Workbook, p. 31, exs 5–7.*

Speaking

Be indecisive! Answer the questions with *might*, giving at least two possibilities.

1 **AT THE BAR:** What are you going to have?
I don't know. I might ... or I might ... or I might even ...
2 **IN THE SHOPS:** What are you going to buy your mum?
3 **BOOKING A FLIGHT:** When are you going to fly?
4 **GOING TO A DINNER PARTY:** What are you going to take as a present?
5 **AT UNIVERSITY:** What subjects are you going to study this year?

A room with a view

Reading

1 Do you ever send e-mails when you are on holiday? Who to? What information do you include?

2 Read this e-mail and answer the questions.

  1 Where is it from? How do you know?

  2 What do you think is Mike's relationship with:
    a) Ben and Tina   b) Georgina?

3 Is the text formal or informal? Explain your answer with examples from the text.

Writing

A postcard

1 Work in pairs.

Student A: Complete the postcard for Raff. He's on holiday in Brazil.
Student B: Complete the postcard for Sarah. She's teaching English in Rome.

Use a word or phrase from each pair in the box.

> beach / teaching
> surfing / language
> guided tour / camping trip
> students / waves
> Tuscany / the jungle
> ~~cappuccino / caipirinha~~

2 Imagine you are in another country, either working or on holiday. Write a postcard to your friends or family.

Vocabulary

Hotel room facilities

1 Match the two columns.

1	private	a)	service
2	internet	b)	TV
3	satellite	c)	conditioning
4	air	d)	bar
5	room	e)	bathroom
6	en suite	f)	terrace
7	sea	g)	connection
8	mini	h)	views

2 When you stay in a hotel, which of these facilities are important to you?

To: bentina@btinternet.co.uk
CC:
Subject: Wish you were here
Attachments: photo1.jpg

Hi! Having a lovely time here. Photo attached. Went surfing yesterday – waves fantastic. As for the tapas, the fried fish is just amazing. Georgina loves that, of course! Tomorrow we're going to cross the Straits. It'll be strange to be in a different continent. Still, it's only 14km from here. Hope you're both OK and Mum and Dad are fine. We'll bring you back an exotic present from Africa!

Miss you lots.
Love
Mike

Hi everybody!

So far, so good ... Having a great time here. I'm sitting in a café drinking an authentic ¹ <u>cappuccino/caipirinha</u> – they're much better than in England! Really enjoying the ²_____ – the ³_____ are fantastic. I'm doing very well with my ⁴_____ course. It's really not so difficult to learn. I'm going on a ⁵_____ in ⁶_____ at the weekend with some friends. I'll send you another card from there.

Well, take care, and I'll write again soon.

Love Raff / Sarah

Useful language

Customer

I'd like to book …
I was looking for …
Does the room have …?
What other facilities are there?
How much is it?
Can I ring back to confirm?
I'll take it.

Receptionist

Can I help you?
Let me see / check.
Could you leave a deposit of …?

TAKEAWAY ENGLISH: *Booking a hotel*

Julie and Jeanette want a hotel on the coast of Ireland for a few nights. Julie is looking for a comfortable room with sea views. Jeanette doesn't mind being further from the sea; she would prefer somewhere cheap but with a mini bar.

1 (5.10) Listen to their conversations at three hotels and complete the table.

	How much is a double room per night?	Is breakfast included?	What facilities are there?
Shannon Hotel			
Murphy's Hotel	49 euros		
Atlantic Hotel			air conditioning, …

2 Which hotel do you think they should choose? Why?

3 (5.11) They phone to make a reservation at one of the hotels. What was the problem?

4 Listen again and complete the conversation.

R: Hello, <u>can</u> _____ _____ _____?
JE: Yes, I called earlier. _____ _____ _____ a double room for next weekend.
R: Certainly, madam. _____ _____ _____ a 10% deposit on the room with a credit card?
JE: Of course. How much was the room again?
R: Er, _____ _____ _____ … 95 euros, in total.
JE: You told us it would be 85!
R: That offer has finished, madam.
JE: Oh. _____ _____ _____ a mini bar though?
R: Yes, all the rooms have a mini bar.
JE: OK, _____ _____ the reservation anyway. Thanks. My visa number is …

5 Work in pairs.

Student A: Turn to page 119.
Student B: Turn to page 121.

Act out a dialogue. Use the Useful language above left to help you.

6 Food to go

- Comparatives and superlatives
- First conditional
- Fast food
- Recipe words
- /u/ & /ʊ/
- Ordering food

Fast food, junk food

Speaking & Reading

1 Discuss these questions.

1 What is junk food? Write down some examples.
2 Is fast food the same as junk food?
3 Why is junk food becoming so popular these days?
4 Where can you eat fast food in your town?
5 Would you ever eat anything like the 'Full Monty'?

2 Do the questionnaire then turn to the key on page 119. Do you agree with the results? What kinds of people are A, B or C?

ARE YOU A JUNK FOOD FREAK?

1 Where do you usually eat lunch?
A At home.
B It depends. Sometimes out and sometimes at home.
C In a sandwich bar or fast food restaurant.

2 What do you normally have for lunch?
A A full three-course meal.
B It depends. Sometimes a full meal and sometimes a sandwich.
C Whatever I can find in the fridge.

3 How often do you have breakfast standing up?
A Never.
B Sometimes.
C Very often.

4 How often do you go to a fast food restaurant (e.g. McDonald's)?
A Only in absolute emergencies.
B From time to time – if I'm in a hurry.
C Often. It's quicker and more fun than eating at home or in a traditional restaurant.

5 Is fast food good for you?
A No. Most of it has no nutritional value at all.
B Some things like sandwiches are OK.
C I don't care about that. I like the taste and that's the important thing.

6 How often do you have snacks like crisps or chocolate bars between meals?
A Not very often. Perhaps if I'm travelling.
B Often. They give you energy when you need it.
C Always. The temptation is too great.

7 Do you ever buy convenience or frozen foods?
A Never. I always cook with fresh ingredients.
B Sometimes, when there's nothing in the fridge.
C All the time. I live on microwave meals.

8 What would you like to have for lunch today?
A A vegetarian salad and grilled fish.
B A Chinese takeaway.
C A hamburger and French fries.

Try the internet activities for this unit at www.webframework.net.

3 Match the shopping receipts to A, B or C people.
Then think of a few more items to add to each list.

①

Fish fingers	£1.49
Frozen pizza	£2.99
Häagen-Dazs ice cream	£1.80
Pringles	£0.92
Chocolate chip cookies	£0.45

_____

_____

②

Organic carrots 1.2 kilos	£0.80
Fresh orange juice	£1.25
Skimmed milk	£0.38
Low fat yoghurt	£1.29
Apples 0.8 kilos	£0.93

_____

_____

③

Spaghetti	£1.05
Sliced white bread	£0.56
Microwave meal	£2.49
6 cans of beer	£5.99
Bananas 1.4 kilos	£1.35

_____

_____

Vocabulary & Listening
Fast food

1 Which ingredients do you associate with these fast foods? Put the words into the correct column. Some words can go in more than one column.

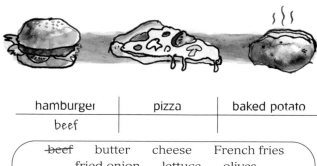

hamburger	pizza	baked potato
beef		

~~beef~~   butter   cheese   French fries
fried onion   lettuce   olives
sesame seed bun   tomato ketchup   tuna

2 (6.1) Listen to a food expert. Which of the ingredients in exercise 1 does she mention for each type of fast food?

3 Listen again and complete the table.

	calories	fat	advice
burger			
pizza			Try pasta
baked potato	Very few		

4 Which is the healthiest food? Which is the least healthy? Is that a surprise?

5 Test your memory. Complete the extracts from the recording with these adjectives.

> best   ~~healthier~~   least healthy
> most popular   much better

1 A good, standard burger is a lot <u>healthier</u> than you imagine.
2 I imagine pizzas are _____ for you than hamburgers.
3 One of the _____ dishes these days is the pizza.
4 This makes the pizza one of the _____ fast foods.
5 The baked potato is definitely the _____ fast food option.

Pronunciation
/u / *food* and /ʊ/ *cook*

1 (6.2) Listen to the sentences. Which word, *cook* or *food*, is pronounced with a longer vowel sound?

She's a great **cook**.
They serve great **food**.

2 Read the information. Then circle the /u / sounds and underline the /ʊ/ sounds in the phrases below.

Cook is pronounced like *put*. It is a shorter sound. /ʊ/
Food is pronounced like *school*. It is a longer sound. /u /

1 a beautiful soup
2 fast food is good for you
3 a superb menu
4 wonderful mushrooms
5 unusual fruit

3 (6.3) Listen and check. Practise saying the phrases.

Death by chocolate

Speaking & Reading

1 Discuss these questions.

1 Are you addicted to any foods or drinks?
2 How long have you been addicted?
3 How much do you eat / drink of this product every day?
4 Do you like chocolate? How much of it do you eat and in what form?

2 Do you think these facts about chocolate are true or false?

1 Women buy less chocolate than men.
2 There is evidence that chocolate is addictive.
3 Chocolate raises your blood cholesterol levels and gives you spots (acne).
4 Chocolate contains caffeine.
5 You should avoid chocolate if you suffer from migraines.
6 The world's greatest chocolate eaters are the British.

Read the article and check your answers. Rewrite the false sentences.

3 Which fact do you find most surprising?

CHOCOHOLICS

Everybody loves chocolate. A cup of cocoa before going to bed or a Mars bar on the bus – the British are obsessed with it. The average Briton eats 10kg of chocolate a year. Women eat far more chocolate than men, an amazing 67% of total chocolate consumption. And the most popular snack is KitKat – fifty are eaten every second in the UK.

Chocoholics are people with a chocolate obsession. But are they addicts? Not according to recent research. This shows that chocolate is not as addictive as coffee – in fact, there is no proof that chocolate creates addiction at all. And it's a lot better for you than we thought. Some scientists say that it releases the same chemicals that your body produces when you are in love. Now that can't be a bad thing!

Some more good news – it doesn't raise your cholesterol level or give you acne as people believe, and it can even be good for your teeth! It does, however, contain caffeine and is bad if you get headaches. So the least sensible time to eat it is at night.

The British love chocolate but they are not as obsessed as the Swiss. The Swiss are officially the world's greatest chocolate eaters – but then Swiss chocolate is the best!

Making chocolate: Try exs 1–2 on your CD-Rom.

Language focus
Comparatives and superlatives

Do Workbook exercises 1–2 on page 36.

Comparative sentences

Which sentence has a different meaning from the others?

1 *Coffee is more addictive than chocolate.*
2 *Coffee is as addictive as chocolate.*
3 *Chocolate is not as addictive as coffee.*
4 *Chocolate is less addictive than coffee.*

Complete the rules.

To compare two things that are the same, we use:
as + adjective + ...

To contrast two things, we can use:
• *more / less* + adjective + ...
• *not as* + adjective + ...

Note: We can't use *less* with adjectives that form their comparative with *-er*. ~~*less nice than*~~

We can also compare using *more / less / fewer* + noun + *than*.

*There are **more chocoholics** in Switzerland **than** in the UK.*
*Chocolate has **less caffeine than** coffee.*
*The British eat **fewer Mars bars than** KitKats.*

With uncountable nouns, we use *more* or ....
With plural countable nouns, we use .... or *fewer*.

Superlative sentences

***The least sensible** time to eat chocolate is at night.*
*The Swiss eat **the most** chocolate.*
*Who eats **the fewest** vegetables and **the least** fruit?*

1 *The least* is the opposite of *the* ....
2 With countable nouns, we use *the* ....
3 With uncountable nouns, we use *the* ....

> See Reference Guide, pp. 9–10.
> See Workbook, pp. 36–7, exs 3–6.

Practice

How many sentences can you make comparing ice cream and chocolate?

EXAMPLE: *Chocolate isn't as nice as ice cream.*

Do the same for *beer / coke, McDonald's / Pizza Hut*.

Listening & Vocabulary

1 🔊6.4 Listen to an interview with chocoholic Oliver Penrose and answer the questions.

1 How long has he been a chocoholic?
   Since he was a child.
2 How much chocolate does he eat a day?
3 When does he eat chocolate?
4 Why did he start eating so much?
5 Why does he want to stop?
6 What does he think he should do?

2 Turn to Reference Guide, page 48, and look at transcript 6.4. Find phrasal verbs that mean the same as these definitions.

1 increase (weight) *put on* 4 stop (a habit)
2 reduce (a habit)   5 recover from
3 start (a habit)   (an illness)

Speaking

You are an addict. Decide what you are addicted to (e.g. coffee, shopping). Interview your partner about his / her addiction. Then swap roles.

Useful language

How long have you been ...? (Since ...)
Why did you start?
How much / often do you ...?
Have you ever tried to give it up?

The Real Thing: *far, by far*

1 Look at the examples and answer the questions.

*It's **far** worse when I haven't got much else to do.*
*It was **by far** the most delicious thing I'd ever tasted.*

1 What do *far* and *by far* mean here?
2 Which do we use with comparatives?
3 Which do we use with superlatives?

2 🔊6.5 Listen and complete the sentences.

1 Don't buy fruit here. It's <u>far cheaper</u> at the market.
2 Don't go to work if you're ill. It's _____ to rest.
3 Christmas is _____ time of the year.
4 Take the plane – it's _____ way to get there.

Listen again and mark the stress.

The big diet

Speaking & Reading

1 Discuss these questions.

  1 Do you remember a TV programme called *Big Brother*? What happened in it?

  2 What do you think happens on a TV programme called *The Big Diet*?

2 Read the information on the right and check your answers.

3 Complete the headings with these words.

> LOSERS   WINNER   PLACE
> ~~PLAYERS~~   MISSION   PRESSURE
> PRIZE

4 Which is the best summary of the programme? Which information is false in the other two summaries?

Summary A

12 fat people are locked in an old house where cameras watch them. They have to follow a strict diet and cannot eat any unhealthy food. After 100 days, the TV audience picks the person who they think has lost the most weight.

Summary B

12 very overweight people are trapped in a mansion and their mission is to lose as much weight as possible. The winner is the person who loses the most weight in 100 days. The contest is made more difficult because there is a lot of tempting food in the house.

Summary C

12 people over 100 kilos in weight have to live together in a country house, while TV cameras watch them suffer. They have to eat two kilos of food a week; if they don't, they have to leave the house. The winner is the first person to lose 20 kilos.

THE [1]PLAYERS: 12 overweight people (some weighing over 100 kilos) – six men and six women.

THE [2]_____: To go on an extreme diet. Contestants have to lose approximately two kilos a week. They also have to do strict exercise and gym sessions.

THE LIMIT: The contestants are allowed to consume only 1,200 calories a day.

THE [3]_____: The contestants are trapped in a luxury mansion somewhere in the middle of the countryside.

THE [4]_____: 42 cameras watch their every move and broadcast them 24 hours a day on television and the internet.

THE CHALLENGE: Contestants have to avoid the 'temptation fridge', which is in the house and contains all their favourite snacks like chocolate, ice cream and cakes.

THE [5]_____: If contestants give way to temptation or fail to lose two kilos a week, they have to leave the programme.

THE [6]_____: The person who manages to lose the most weight after 100 days.

THE [7]_____: The winner will receive the weight he / she has lost in gold.

THE CONTROVERSY: Many people have criticised the programme for encouraging anorexia among young people and for promoting the idea that being fat is an essentially bad thing.

Speaking

1 Discuss these questions.

  1 What do you think of programmes like this?
  2 Why do you think they are so popular?
  3 Is there anything wrong with being fat?

2 Look at this advice for losing weight. Do you agree / disagree? Why?

  1 You shouldn't eat meat.
  2 You should have snacks between meals.
  3 You should take up smoking.
  4 You should fall in love.
  5 You shouldn't eat late at night.
  6 You should keep a note of the food you eat.
  7 You should drink lots of water.
  8 You should have an operation.

Remember!
We use *should / shouldn't* + infinitive to give advice.

> *See Reference Guide, pp. 10–11.*
> *See Workbook, p. 37, ex. 7.*

Listening

1 (6.6) Listen to four people talking about losing weight. Match the speakers (1–4) with their pictures (a–d).

2 Listen again. Which advice from Speaking exercise 2 do they mention?

EXAMPLE: 1 – *take up smoking*

Language focus

First conditional

(6.7) Listen and complete the sentences.

1 If you _____ a lot of meat, you _____ fat for sure.
2 If your weight _____ a problem, this _____ you.

> **Complete the rules.**
>
> To form a first conditional sentence, we use:
> *If* + ..., *will* (*'ll*) + infinitive
> The negative of *will* is ....
>
> **Complete this sentence. Use *won't*.**
>
> *If you continue to eat chocolate, you* ....
> ....
>
> > *See Reference Guide, p. 11.*
> > *See Workbook, p. 38, exs 8–9.*

Practice

Complete the first conditional sentences with the correct form of the verb in brackets.

1 If you **drink** (drink) less alcohol, you **'ll get** (get) slimmer.
2 You _____ (feel) better about your body if you _____ (go) to the gym every day.
3 If a new gym _____ (open), I _____ (join) it.
4 If you _____ (be) very overweight, you _____ (not live) as long as slim people.
5 If my mother _____ (start) a diet, she _____ (look) better on the beach this summer.
6 I _____ (not sleep) well tonight if I _____ (not stop) eating chocolate.

Speaking

Work in pairs. Listen to your partner's problem and give him / her advice.

> **Useful language**
>
> You should / shouldn't ...
> Have you thought of ...ing?
> Why don't you ...?
> What about ...ing?
> If you ... , you'll ...

Student A
I can't sleep at night.
I need to learn English fast.
I'm stressed out with work.
I'm worried about my exams.

Student B
I get a lot of bad headaches.
I feel depressed and I can't get out of bed in the morning.
I never have any money.
I find it hard to meet new people.

Eat in or takeaway?

Vocabulary
Recipe words

1 Discuss these questions.

1 Are you a good cook?
2 What recipes do you know?
3 Do you know any typical US or British recipes?

2 Match the pictures (a–f) with verbs from this list. You will not need four of the verbs.

> add   beat   boil   chop   cook
> fry c)   heat   peel   sprinkle   stir

3 Complete the ingredients list for a Spanish omelette for four people.

> _____ large potatoes   A pinch of _____
> _____ onion   1 cup of _____ _____
> _____ eggs

Compare with your partner.

4 Complete the recipe using ingredients and verbs from exercises 2 and 3.

> 1 Peel the <u>potatoes</u> and _____.
> 2 _____ them into small pieces.
> 3 _____ the oil in a frying pan.
> 4 _____ the onion and potatoes slowly on a low heat until the potatoes are done.
> 5 Beat the _____ and salt in a small bowl and _____ the potato and onion mixture.
> 6 _____ everything together and return to the frying pan to cook.
> 7 When it is ready, turn it over and _____ it on the other side.
> 8 Eat and enjoy!

Listening

1 (6.8) Listen to someone telling a friend how to make a well-known dish. Answer the questions.

1 What ingredients does she mention?
   minced meat, ...
2 Is the dish easy or difficult to make?
3 What do you think the recipe is for?

2 Listen again and tick the linking expressions you hear.

> First of all✔   In the first place   To start with
> When that's done   When that's finished
> When that's ready   Next   Then   Finally
>   To finish

Turn to Reference Guide, page 49, transcript 6.8 and check. Compare it to the written recipe in exercise 4. What differences do you notice?

Speaking & Writing
Your own recipe

1 Tell your partner how to cook something. Use linking expressions from Listening exercise 2.

2 Write down your recipe. Use the Spanish omelette recipe to help you.

Put the ingredients first.
List the actions step by step (1, 2, 3 ...)
Use imperatives: Peel ... Chop ...

Pronunciation
Food

1 Look at these words. Which words have the same or very similar spelling in your language?

banana   biscuit   chocolate   fruit cake   ketchup
margarine   sandwich   toffee   vinegar   yoghurt

2 How do you say the words in English? Mark the stress.

(6.9) Listen and check. Which words sound most different from your language?

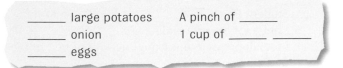

Cooking with chocolate: Try exs 1–6 on your CD-Rom.

TAKEAWAY ENGLISH: *Ordering food*

1 Answer the questions.

1 How often do you eat out?
2 What type of food do you like?
3 Think of your favourite place to eat. Why do you like it so much?

2 (6.10) Listen and complete the questions. Mark the stress and intonation.

1 Are you <u>ready</u> to _____?
2 Can we have the _____, please?
3 Can we see the menu in _____, please?
4 Can I get you anything _____?
5 Would you like to see the _____?

Who is asking each question: the waiter / waitress or the customer?

3 Match questions 1–5 above with answers a–e

a) No, thanks. Just some water, please.
b) Of course, sir. Sorry about that.
c) Yes. I'll have the fried fish ...
d) No, thanks. Just the bill, please.
e) Certainly, sir.

(6.11) Listen and check.

4 (6.12) Listen to three dialogues. What type of restaurant are the people in?

5 Listen again. What does each couple order? Complete the table.

	food	drink
1	enchiladas with cheese/not decided	
2		
3		

6 In pairs, practise ordering food in a restaurant.

Student A: You are the waiter / waitress at Café Deco.
Student B: You are a customer at Café Deco.

CAFÉ DECO

MENU

Starters
Avocado salad
Melon with ham
Carrot and coriander soup

Main courses
Cod and chips
Vegetarian pie
Lamb moussaka

Desserts
Chocolate cake
Homemade apple pie
Strawberries and cream

Useful language

Waiter / waitress
Are you ready to order?
Can I take your order?
Would you like to see the wine list?
Can I get you anything else?

Customer
I'll have the lamb moussaka.
I'd like an avocado salad.
Can I have cream with the apple pie?

Now do Unit test 6 on your CD-Rom.

The *Cinnamon Club*

Iqbal

Vox pops

[07:35-08:28] Watch the vox pops and answer the on-screen questions.

1 Watch again. Who says it?

1 I think it'll have to be Italian food.
2 I like French food.
3 My favourite food in the world is sushi.

2 Test your memory. Complete the gaps.

IQBAL: I _____ _____ four times a week.
TRAVIS: Probably _____ a week …
LUKE: Once in a _____ moon.

Watch again and check your answers.

Before you watch

1 Discuss in pairs.

1 What's your favourite type of food?
2 How often do you eat out?
3 Where's your favourite place to eat? Why do you like it?

2 Which of these adjectives would you use to describe the food where you live?

> delicious   fast   fattening   healthy
> home-made   simple   sophisticated
> spicy   varied

What are the typical local dishes where you live?

3 The *Cinnamon Club* is a restaurant. What type of restaurant do you think it is?

> **cinnamon** /ˈsɪnəmən/ (n): a brown spice which comes from the bark of a tree. It comes in a brown powder or small stick.

While you watch

Sequence 1 [08:29-10:05]

Iqbal Wahhab is the owner of the *Cinnamon Club*, a new restaurant in the heart of London.

Watch sequence 1 and answer the questions.

1 What do these numbers refer to? Make sentences.

1 11 months = The restaurant opened 11 months ago
2 230
3 2000
4 1894

2 The building was originally …

a) a shop   b) a nightclub   c) a library

3 Circle the correct answer.

a) When did Iqbal's family come over to Britain?
   1964 / 1968 / 1974

b) How old was Iqbal when they arrived?
   8 months / 12 months / 18 months

c) What did his parents do? They were …
   journalists / restaurateurs / academics

Watch again and check.

Sequence 2 [10:06-11:28]

Watch sequence 2 and answer the questions.

1 Where does Iqbal want to open other new restaurants? Tick the cities you hear.

| Amsterdam | Athens | Berlin | Bombay |
| Dublin✓ | London | New York | Paris |

2 At lunchtime, the *Cinnamon Club* serves a lot of …

a) students   b) Members of Parliament   c) celebrities

3 In the evening, the *Cinnamon Club* serves a lot of …

a) business people   b) media people   c) TV personalities

Sequence 3 [11:29-13:10]

■ [11:29-12:12] Watch part 1 of sequence 3 and answer the questions.

1 How often does the *Cinnamon Club* change its menu?

2 Iqbal says that British cuisine …

a) … is still quite traditional.
b) … is a mixture of all the world's cuisines.
c) … has changed a lot in recent years.

3 Iqbal talks about going out to eat in London. Which nationalities does he mention? Tick the words you hear.

> Bangladeshi   Belgian   Brazilian
> Egyptian   Eritrean   Ethiopian✓
> French   Indian   Italian

4 ■ [12:13-13:10] Now watch the rest of the sequence. Listen to the chef and complete the gaps.

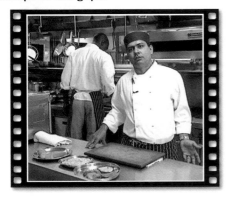

We opened the *Cinnamon Club* in ¹_____ last year after long, long delays. I'm here from ²_____ every morning up until, you know, the end of the night, six days or ³_____ days a week. We've got Tandoori ovens which are like clay ovens which are coal-fired and they go up to ⁴_____ of 250° to 350° centigrade – really, really fired and, you know, hot.

Watch the whole DVD again and answer the on-screen questions.

After you watch

Can you remember? Tick the furniture and objects that you see in the *Cinnamon Club*.

> a bar   bookcases   a bowl of petals
> a fountain   an Indian carpet   a mirror
> a painting   a plant   a staircase
> velvet curtains

World culture:

Herbs and spices

Without herbs and spices, our food would be very boring! The herbs and spices that we use every day come from all over the world.

1 Find these herbs and spices in the wordsearch. (Words may be horizontal, vertical or diagonal.)

cinnamon   garlic   mustard

C	I	N	N	A	M	O	N	L	L
M	O	U	H	V	I	F	S	V	T
U	J	R	P	G	N	A	B	A	J
S	R	A	E	C	T	C	K	N	R
T	M	I	P	G	A	R	L	I	C
A	F	S	P	O	A	V	G	P	H
R	H	T	E	O	Z	N	U	L	F
D	D	L	R	R	J	T	O	A	D
N	O	P	P	A	R	G	L	E	Y

mint   pepper   oregano

2 Match each herb or spice with a definition.

1 This comes from Asia and has a strong, sweet flavour with a cool aftertaste. It is used in salads, Moroccan tea and toothpaste.

2 This is a seed. The French add it to cold meats and cheeses, and the Americans put it in hamburgers.

3 This spice comes from Sri Lanka. It is used in cakes and biscuits and you can put it on top of cappuccino coffee.

4 A dried leaf with a strong smell. It is used in lots of Italian foods, especially pizza.

5 This spice has been available since Roman times. There are three main types: green, white and black. It comes from India and Brazil.

6 This is a round white vegetable but it is used as a spice in the form of a dry powder. It has a very strong smell and flavour and is essential in the Mediterranean diet.

Flashback 2

Vocabulary & Speaking

1 Work in pairs. Write three words / phrases in each category. Who finishes first in your class?

1 Sports you play in a team – football, …
2 Things you can use as a pizza topping
3 Sports you can do on your own
4 Things you need in the mountains
5 Things you need to play tennis
6 Things you should do to lose weight
7 Things you take on a cruise
8 Things you do on a city holiday
9 Places where sports are played
10 Ways of preparing food
11 Ingredients of a Spanish omelette
12 Things you wear to go swimming

Look at Units 4–6 to check your answers.

2 *a* Match the nouns with the verbs below.

> ~~football~~ athletics sightseeing holiday
> a diet swimming camping jog skiing
> bike ride tennis golf cycling yoga a trip
> windsurfing basketball exercise aerobics

play football,   go …   do …   go for a …   go on …

b 'Collocation Snap'. Write verbs and nouns on pieces of paper and divide into two piles. Turn over verbs and nouns until the noun matches the verb. 'Snap!'

Language focus

1 *a* Work in pairs.

Student A: Read the lifeguard notes.
Student B: Read the teacher notes.

Use *have to / don't have to / must / can / can't / should / shouldn't* to write job descriptions.

EXAMPLE: You have to watch the swimming pool all the time.

b Tell your partner about the job.

c Write a description of another job. Read it to other students. Can they guess what the job is?

Lifeguard

prohibited – leave the pool unattended
necessary – watch the swimming pool all the time
not necessary – stay in the lifeguard's chair
possible – walk around the pool
not possible – swim or train while working
a good idea – pay extra attention to children
not a good idea – listen to music or read

Primary school teacher

prohibited – send children home early
necessary – arrive fifteen minutes before the class begins
not necessary – look after children during the lunch break
possible – take children on school trips twice a year
not possible – take holidays during the school term
a good idea – do projects with the children
not a good idea – give a lot of homework

2 a Write down your plans for the next ten years. Use *going to* and *might*. Use these ideas to help you.

EXAMPLE: I'm going to change jobs.

> fall in love   learn to speak Greek
> change jobs   go and live in another country
> work in television   become famous
> work in an office   win the lottery   buy a flat
> study abroad   go on holiday to Cuba

b In pairs, make predictions about your partner's life in the next ten years. Use *will* and *might*.

EXAMPLE: I think she'll change jobs.

c Compare your predictions to your partner's plans.

3 a Discuss these questions.

1 Where's your favourite restaurant?
2 What type of places do you like?

b Look at the advertisements for three restaurants. Write sentences comparing them. Use the words below to help you.

> big   cheap   comfortable   convenient
> early   exotic   expensive   late   small
> tasty   traditional   trendy

EXAMPLE: Take Sushi is trendier than Gino's.
Gino's isn't as expensive as Take Sushi.

c Work in groups. Which of the restaurants would you prefer and why?

GINO'S

Pasta & pizza

The biggest pizzas in town at the best prices – from €10.

Seating for 30 people.

Open 7 pm – 2 am.

Take Sushi

Japanese restaurant

Specialities: **sushi and sashimi**

From €15

Located in the Aciria cinema complex.

Open 8 pm – midnight daily.

STEAK & SALAD

Tasty grilled steaks and hamburgers.

Self-service salad bar.

Seating for 50 people. Large groups welcome!

Prices start at €20.

Open 1 pm to 4 pm and 7 pm to 11 pm.

Listening

1 a (F2.1) Listen to the conversation. Which of the restaurants in Exercise 3 are the people in?

b Listen again and write down the orders.

I salad

c Listen again and write down the phrases they use to order their food.

Turn to Reference Guide, page 50, transcript F2.1, to check your answers.

You *choose!*

1 a You are a holiday company rep. Prepare a welcome speech for a group of tourists. Include the following:

- What the weather will be like
- What they'll do during their stay
- Places they'll visit
- Things they might eat and drink

b Give your welcome speech to your classmates. Answer any questions they have.

OR

2 Work in groups of five. Role-play the following situation.

Student A: You've finished school and you're trying to decide what to do next.
Student B: You're A's friend. You play together in a band. You think you should try to become professional musicians.
Student C: You're A's boyfriend / girlfriend. You'd like to go travelling together for a year.
Student D: You're A's teacher. You think A should go to university.
Student E: You're A's mother / father. You work in an office and can get A a job there.

Who is the most persuasive?

OR

3 a Work in groups. You're going to open a restaurant where you live. Plan your restaurant. Think about …

- the menu   • the décor   • the location
- the opening times   • prices

b Present your proposal to the class. Take a class vote on the best restaurant.

7 Money talks

- Passive voice – present & past
- Present Perfect with *just* & *already*
- Money collocations
- *Make & do*
- /ɒ/ & /ə/
- Money problems

Spend, spend, spend!

Vocabulary
Money collocations

1 What do you spend your money on? What would you like to spend it on?

2 Match the two columns. There is more than one correct answer.

bet money	in a bank account
borrow money	on cigarettes
earn money	on clothes
invest money	from a friend
save money	on a horse race
spend money	on the lottery
waste money	in property
win money	at work

3 Complete the sentences and then compare with your partner.

I waste a lot of money on _____ but I don't spend much money on _____.

I like to save about _____ % of the money I have.

Sometimes I borrow money from _____.

I once won / lost a lot of money on _____.

I'd like to buy a _____ but I can't afford it.

Money collocations: Try exs 1–3 on your CD-Rom.

Reading

1 Are you generous or mean? Do you like to save or do you spend extravagantly?

2 Do the questionnaire and then look at the key on page 121. Do you agree with the results?

3 In pairs, write two more multiple-choice questions for the questionnaire. Choose from these topics.

> buying food   choosing a holiday
> saving   taking a taxi

ARE YOU MEAN WITH MONEY?

1 Do you shop for clothes in the sales?

A Almost never. The clothes I like aren't usually in the sales.

B Always. Clothes are too expensive otherwise.

C Sometimes. It depends if I can find a bargain.

2 How much do you leave as a tip after a good meal in an expensive restaurant?

A 10%, or more if the waiters were really nice.

B I never leave a tip. Waiters earn enough money anyway.

C It depends on the service but I usually leave some coins.

3 A good friend needs to borrow money to pay his / her rent. What do you do?

A Give him / her the money without asking questions.

B Don't lend him / her anything, because I might never get it back.

C Lend the money if it's really important.

4 A homeless person stops you in the street and asks you for money. What do you do?

A Give some money, even if it's only a little.

B Walk past without giving anything. I don't think it helps these people.

C It depends. I sometimes give money if the person looks ill or very thin.

5 Your favourite pop group is doing a concert in your town but the only tickets left are really expensive. What do you do?

A Buy a ticket anyway.

B Save my money. I can watch the concert on TV for free.

C Go and buy a CD of their music instead.

6 It's your grandmother's 75th birthday. What do you give her?

A Something that she would really like. It doesn't matter how much it costs.

B An old present that someone gave me but that I didn't like.

C Something special if I can afford it.

Listening

1 What have you spent money on in the last week?

2 (7.1) Listen to three people's answers to the question above. Who is the most careful with money? Who is the most extravagant?

3 Listen again and complete the table.

	What did they spend their money on?	Was it expensive?
Joey	1 Food	No
	2	
	3	
Boris	1	
	2	
	3	
Natalie	1	
	2	
	3	

The Real Thing: *I suppose / I guess*

You use *I suppose / I guess* when you reflect on something or you are not sure about it.

1 (7.2) Listen and complete the sentences.

Well, I guess I spend a lot of my money on music.
Yes, _____ I'm very careful with money.
That's where the money really goes, _____.
I also like expensive things, _____.

2 (7.3) Now listen and complete these dialogues.

1 A: Do you want to earn more money?
   B: I guess so.
2 A: Can you help me do the washing up?
   B: I _____.

Mark the stress on the missing words.

3 In pairs, practise dialogues using *guess* and *suppose*. Use these prompts to help you.

> carry my bag   lend me money
> like your job   live in a nice place

EXAMPLE:
A: Could you lend me some money until Friday?
B: I suppose so. How much do you need? ...

63

Market leaders

jeans · mobiles · soft drinks · hamburgers

Speaking & Reading

1 Answer the questions.

1 What companies do you associate with the products above?
2 Do you know which company is the market leader in your country?
3 Is the same company market leader in the world?

2 Guess the correct answer.

1 McDonald's was founded in:
 a) New York b) California c) Texas
2 Coca-Cola was invented by:
 a) a pharmacist b) a doctor c) a nutritionist
3 Nokia is based in:
 a) Japan b) Korea c) Finland
4 The first pair of Levi's jeans were made in:
 a) 1853 b) 1873 c) 1903

3 Now read the text and check your answers.

4 Test your partner's memory. What do these numbers refer to (two per product)?

8 hours	45 million	1886	200 million
¼	1991	1960s	2%

Make sentences.

EXAMPLE: A new McDonald's restaurant opens every eight hours.

5 Discuss these questions.

1 How often do you eat fast food? Do you ever go to McDonald's?
2 Do you drink Coca-Cola or do you prefer Pepsi? How much coke do you drink?
3 Have you got a Nokia mobile now or have you owned one in the past? Do you like mobiles? Why / Why not?
4 Do you think Levi's are the best jeans? How many pairs of jeans do you have?

The hamburger was invented in 1889, and the first McDonald's <u>opened</u> in 1948 in San Bernadino, California. Now a new McDonald's restaurant opens every eight hours somewhere in the world. The restaurant chain <u>serves</u> about 45 million customers every day. The corporation's yellow and red M <u>is recognised</u> by people all over the world as a symbol of dynamism, happiness and, above all, America. The busiest restaurant, however, is in Moscow.

Coca-Cola is the most successful product in history and today it is sold in 185 countries. The drink was invented in 1886 by pharmacist John Pemberton in Atlanta, Georgia, while he was trying to stop his addiction to morphine. It is estimated that 200 million cans or bottles of coke <u>are sold</u> every 24 hours. 80% of Coca-Cola's profits now <u>come</u> from outside the United States.

Language focus
Passive voice – present and past

> **Look at the examples and complete the rules.**
>
> *Coca-Cola is sold in 185 countries.*
> To form the Present Simple passive, we use the present tense of the verb .... + past participle.
>
> *Coca-Cola was invented by John Pemberton.*
> To form the Past Simple passive, we use the past tense of the verb .... + ...
>
> We can use the passive voice when it is not important (or we don't know) who did the action.
>
> *Coca-Cola is sold in 185 countries.* (no object or agent)
>
> Find a similar example in the text.
>
> ....
>
> If it is important who did the action, we use .... to show who the agent is.
>
> <u>*Coca-Cola*</u> *was invented by* <u>*John Pemberton*</u>.
>   subject   agent
>
> Find a similar example in the text.
>
> ....
>
> How do you say the examples above in your language?
>
> ....
> ....
>
> *See Reference Guide, pp. 11–12.*
> *See Workbook, p. 45–6, exs 1–5.*

Practice

1 Look at the verbs <u>underlined</u> in the text below. Which are in the passive voice?

2 Complete the sentences with the correct form of the verb in brackets – Past Simple or Present Simple, active or passive.

1 Nowadays, 25% of the world's cars <u>are made</u> (make) in Asia.
2 Before 1980, most Levi's jeans _____ (produce) in the USA.
3 In the 1980s, Levi Strauss _____ (open) a lot of jeans factories in Latin America and Asia.
4 86% of the world's goods _____ (use) by 20% of the world's population.
5 Half the world – nearly 3 billion people – _____ (live) on $2 a day.
6 Over a quarter of the world's goods _____ (produce) by 200 multinational companies.
7 In 1999, more than half a million people _____ (demonstrate) in Seattle in an anti-globalisation march.

3 Which of the sentences above give good or bad news? Why? (Some are neutral.)

Ironically, the Nokia Corporation <u>started</u> life as a paper manufacturer – the original form of communication. Nearly 150 years later, this Finnish company is the world's largest mobile phone producer and accounts for more than a quarter of Finland's total economy. Nokia was the pioneer of mobile phone communication. In fact, the first text message <u>was sent</u> by the mayor of Helsinki on a Nokia mobile in 1991.

The Levi Strauss company <u>was founded</u> in 1853 and twenty years later they produced their first pair of jeans. The trousers <u>were designed</u> as tough, long-lasting workclothes for the workers of San Francisco. In the 1960s, blue jeans <u>became</u> very popular and since then they have never gone out of fashion. It is estimated that Levi Strauss now make approximately 2% of the world's clothes.

Anti-globalisation

Speaking & Reading

1 Discuss these questions.

  1 Do you know the name of the US flag?

  2 Look carefully at the version of the flag below. What do you think it represents? Do you know any of the logos?

  3 Who do you think first used this flag? When and where?

2 Read the text and check your answers.

3 Answer the questions.

  1 Why do you think the flag is called the 'Brands and Bands'?

  2 What are anti-globalisation demonstrators protesting about?

  3 Do you think their protests do any good?

  4 Are there any products or brands that you don't buy? Why not?

4 These are the opinions of some Americans on the Corporate America flag. Who is in favour of the flag?

> It's shocking to make fun of our national flag like this.

> It's a great way to make people aware of the problem.

> Sadly it won't have any effect on the general public.

> I have no idea what it means, but it's cool!

> It's offensive and an insult to all Americans.

Vocabulary

Make and do

1 In the exercises on the left we saw the expressions *make fun of something / someone* and *do some good*. Complete these expressions with *make* or *do*.

  1 __do__ some good   5 _____ money

  2 _____ your best   6 _____ damage

  3 _____ a mess   7 _____ business

  4 _____ a difference   8 _____ progress

2 Complete the interview between a protestor and a journalist. Use words from exercise 1.

J: Do you really think your protests make a [1]*difference*?

P: Yes, I do. If enough people join our movement, we can change the way that big corporations do [2]_____. At the moment, North America and Western Europe make a lot of [3]_____ in the poor countries of the world, but they don't use this money to help the people there. We have to do our [4]_____ to stop this.

J: But don't you agree that violent protests, like the one in Seattle, do a lot of [5]_____ to your campaign? Protesters make a [6]_____ in the streets, with graffiti and broken glass. People get angry with you. How does this help you to make [7]_____?

P: If we can do some [8]_____ in the world, a few broken windows don't matter.

This is the Corporate America flag – the 'Brands and Bands'. It is a symbol of the anti-globalisation movement. The flag was first used in demonstrations across the United States on July 4th 2001, the USA's Independence Day, as a symbol of how crazy this consumerist world has become.

Listening

1  **(7.4)** In December 1999, the first major anti-globalisation protest took place in Seattle. Listen to this news report and answer the questions.

1 Are the police and the demonstrators fighting at the moment?

2 Which four companies are mentioned in the report?

> Burger King   McDonald's   Netscape
> Microsoft   Starbucks✓   Benetton
> Boeing   IBM

3 Which two people does the correspondent interview?

> a police officer   a protester
> a conference delegate

2 Listen again and answer true (T) or false (F).

1 The windows of Starbucks are smashed.

2 The police used tear gas and rubber bullets on the protesters.

3 Jenny Peterson has already done a day's work.

4 The mayor of Seattle has just declared a state of emergency.

Language focus

Present Perfect with *just* and *already*

Look at the examples and complete the rules.

Jenny Peterson has already done a day's work.
The mayor of Seattle has just declared a state of emergency.

These sentences are in the Present Perfect. We form the Present Perfect with .... + past participle.

We use *have* + ... + past participle to describe something that was completed recently, perhaps sooner than expected.

We use *have* + ... + past participle to describe a very recent event.

How do you say these sentences in your language?

We've already finished. ....
He has just arrived. ....

> *See Reference Guide, p.13.*
> *See Workbook, p. 46, exs 6–7.*

Practice

Complete the sentences in the Present Perfect.

1 I <u>have just written</u> (just / write) to the government about working conditions in Pakistan.

2 He _____ (already / interview) a protester and now he wants to interview a police officer.

3 They _____ (just / arrest) a man for painting graffiti on the pavement.

4 Someone _____ (just / break) the windows in my office.

5 The delegates _____ (already / leave) the conference.

Pronunciation

/ɒ/ *hot* and /ʌ/ *son*

1 The *o* in English is not always pronounced as in *hot*. Look at the first syllable of each word. Where is it pronounced like *hot* and where like *son*?

coffee   colour   dollar   gossip   government
London   lovely   money   office   orange
sorry   worry

(7.5) Listen and check.

2 **(7.6)** Listen and repeat. Practise saying the sentences.

1 There's not a lot of money left for our trip to London.

2 Did you hear the gossip about the government?

3 Sorry, I forgot to pay for my coffee.

4 Don't worry. It's only two dollars!

5 Look at the sky! It's a lovely orange colour.

Status symbols

Speaking & Listening

1 Work in pairs. Make a list of places where you see advertising.

EXAMPLE: in the street, in magazines ...

Are there any products which can't be advertised?

2 Look at adverts a and b above and describe each one.

1 What is the image?
2 What do you think it is advertising?

Turn to page 124 and look at the complete adverts. Were you right?

3  Listen to two marketing students describing the adverts. Answer the questions.

1 Which advert is he / she describing?
2 Who is it targeted at?
3 What is the message?

4 Describe the advert on the right.

> **Useful language**
>
> The advert shows ...
> It is advertising ...
> It is targeted at ...
> I think the message is ...

www.tagheuer.com

BEYOND MEASURE

TAGHeuer
SWISS MADE SINCE 1860

SERIE KIRIUM

Writing
Adverts

Look at the photos and complete the adverts using these expressions. Then invent a slogan.

~~a new look~~   class and elegance
number one   pure gold   our wide range
speed and comfort   spring collection
unrepeatable offer

Wear the best sunglasses money can buy.

A new look for this summer. Choose from _____ of frames and colours. You won't regret it.

Ray-Ban: LOOK GOOD IN THE SUN!

Ray-Ban

A watch that will last a lifetime.

Made from quartz and _____. A sign of _____, wherever you go.

Viceroy: _____!

Drive the best car on earth, combining _____ at a fantastic price. Make the most of this _____. You'll never get the chance again.

Jaguar: _____ !

Italy's _____ fashion label has arrived! Be the first to try our new _____. Classic cuts and cool elegance.

Dress the part with Armani.

Armani: _____ !

1 (7.8) Listen and match the dialogues (1–4) with the pictures (a–d).

2 (7.9) Listen to these requests and responses again. Complete the sentences.

1 '_____ the bill, please?' 'Yes, of course.'
2 '_____ breakfast brought to room 209, please?' 'Straight away, madam.'
3 '_____ by credit card?' 'Sure, just one moment.'
4 '_____ holding the line?' 'Well, OK.'
5 '_____ some money, please.' 'Certainly, sir.'
6 '_____ some tickets for tonight's show, please?' 'No problem.'

Which of these requests is not made by the customer?

3 The customers are having problems. Match the apologies and excuses they are given (1–4) with the pictures above (a–d).

1 I'm sorry, sir. We're having problems with the line.
2 Sorry about the confusion. Now, how much did you want to change?
3 OK, I'll see what I can do. I'm afraid we're short of staff tonight.
4 I'm terribly sorry, but there's nothing here for 209.

(7.10) Listen and check.

4 In pairs, choose a place from pictures a–d. The customer has a problem. Act out the conversation.

EXAMPLE:
A: Can I have the bill, please?
B: Certainly, sir ...
(Ten minutes later ...)

8 Gossip

- Past Perfect
- *see, watch, look at*
- The press
- /h/
- Gossiping

Stars in their eyes

	Name	Why are they famous?	Where are they from?	Are they alive or dead?
a)				
b)	Karen Carpenter	She's a singer.		
c)				
d)				
e)				
f)				
g)				
h)				
i)				

Speaking & Listening

1 In pairs, look at the photos and complete the table.

2 Swap partners and compare your answers.

3 (8.1) Listen to three conversations. Which celebrities are the people talking about?

The Real Thing: ***don't you think? isn't he?***

1 (8.2) Listen and complete the sentences.

He's still really attractive, _____? She's from Australia, _____?
And she's incredibly beautiful, _____? She's a better actor than he is, _____?

Why do we use these expressions? What would you say in your language?

NOTE: We only use *isn't he / she / it?* with the verb *to be*.

2 (8.3) Listen to three conversations and answer the questions for each one.

1 What are they talking about?
2 Which of the above expressions did you hear?

3 Work in pairs. Talk about another celebrity. Try to use the new expressions.

EXAMPLE: Do you like Will Smith? He's really sexy, don't you think?...

Reading & Vocabulary

1 Read about three musicians and match them with the photos of their fans. Turn to page 122.

2 In groups, decide which of the three – John Lennon, Karen Carpenter or Kurt Cobain:

1 wasn't born in the United States.
2 died under the age of 30.
3 played music with his / her brother.
4 was famous in the 60s.
5 had an eating disorder.
6 was married to a famous singer.

3 Write questions for these answers.

1 10 million copies.   3 32 years old.
2 In New York.   4 One daughter.

4 What did the three musicians have in common? Complete the sentences, using the past participles of these verbs.

> be   ~~become~~   have   make   spend   write

When they died …

1 … they had all _become_ very famous.
2 … they had all _____ lots of records.
3 … they had all _____ big hits in the charts.
4 … they had all _____ married.
5 … they had all _____ a lot of time in the USA.
6 … they had all _____ some great songs.

Which of these sentences is false?

Language focus
Past Perfect

Look at the example and complete the rule.

*When they died, they **had made** lots of records.*

To form the Past Perfect, we use the verb _____ + _____.

We use the Past Perfect to show that one action happened <u>before</u> another in the past.

```
                          die
    |——— make records ———|————→ present
 earlier past           past
```

The contraction of *had* is *'d*. Be careful not to confuse it with *'d = would*.

Match the sentences (1–3) with the pictures (a–c).

1 When I got home, my mother had supper.
2 When I got home, my mother was having supper.
3 When I got home, my mother had had supper.

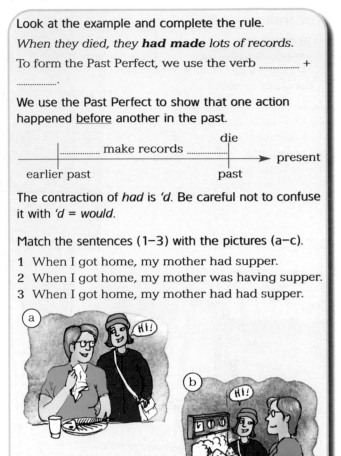

> *See Reference Guide, p.13.*
> *See Workbook, pp. 51–2, exs 1–5.*

Practice

Complete the sentences in the Past Perfect.

> ask   drink   leave   ~~lose~~   win   work

1 He had no money because he _had lost_ his job the month before.
2 He was depressed because his wife _____ him for a divorce.
3 She was worried because her daughter _____ home without warning.
4 He was sick because he _____ too much beer.
5 She was excited because she _____ a lot of money on the lottery.
6 Before she became famous, she _____ in a café.

Famous people: Try exs 1–2 on your CD-Rom.

Paparazzi

Vocabulary

The press

Match the words (1–6) with items in the pictures (a–f).

1 an article
2 a broadsheet newspaper
3 a headline
4 a magazine
5 the paparazzi
6 a tabloid newspaper

EXAMPLE: 1 – f

Speaking

Discuss these questions.

1 Who are the most photographed celebrities in your country?
2 Can you think of celebrity scandals that have taken place recently?
3 How do you find out about celebrity gossip?
4 What sort of photographs do the paparazzi take?
5 Some people think that the paparazzi and the newspapers that publish their photos are immoral. Do you agree? Why / Why not?

Listening & Vocabulary

A day in the life of a paparazzo

1 Look at the three pictures. Imagine the story that they tell.

2 (8.4) Listen to a paparazzo talking about his day. Answer the questions. Did you get the story right?

1 Who does the paparazzo phone?
2 Who does he see?
3 Does he get a good photo in the end?
4 Why does he have to hurry?
5 How does he feel at the end? Why?

3 Complete the text with the correct form of these verbs. Use the Present Simple.

> chase   feel   ~~get~~   hide   look   need
> phone   see   smile   watch

Sunday

9am: I ¹ get a call from Pepe at La Gaviota in Marbella.

10am: I ² _____ my editor to check the shots that he wants.

11am: I ³ _____ behind the bushes outside La Gaviota.

1pm: I ⁴ _____ the first celebrities arriving.

1.15pm: I ⁵ _____ George Clooney and his new girlfriend. They're in a limousine and I can't get a good shot.

1.20pm: They decide to enter the restaurant via the back door, so I ⁶ _____ after the limousine on my motorbike.

1.25pm: I take a perfect shot of Clooney and his girlfriend arm in arm. He even ⁷ _____ at me!

1.30pm: After fighting with Clooney's bodyguard, I ⁸ _____ at my watch. The newspaper ⁹ _____ the photo now.

1.40pm: At the office, I search for the film, but I don't have it! I ¹⁰ _____ really stupid.

4 Listen again and check.

Vocabulary

see, watch, look at

1 Look at the examples and read the explanation.

I see George Clooney and his new girlfriend.
I watch the first celebrities arriving.
I look at my watch.

> • We see everything that comes in front of our eyes, sometimes without trying.
> • We *watch* a football match, or children playing – usually something that is happening.
> • We *look at* a watch, a timetable, a photo – something that we find useful or interesting. We often use the imperative: *Look at me! Look at that car!*
>
> **Note:** We *watch* television, but we usually *see* a film, a play, a TV programme.

2 Complete the sentences with *see*, *watch* or *look at*.

1 I _____ television last night.
2 They _____ the photos of the wedding. There were some really funny ones!
3 She _____ the procession from her balcony.
4 You can _____ for miles.
5 I waited outside the restaurant for hours but I didn't _____ any celebrities.
6 _____ that cloud! Is it going to rain?

Writing

A paparazzo encounter

Imagine you are a paparazzo. Write about your encounter with a famous person. Use these verbs.

> think   feel   get   hide   look
> remember   phone   see   listen   watch

EXAMPLE: I was watching Penelope Cruz from behind the bushes. Suddenly ...

Speaking

Do you agree with these statements?

1 Hollywood film stars and other celebrities are paid too much.
2 The private lives of famous people are interesting.
3 People enjoy hearing about famous people's problems because they are jealous of their success.
4 It is wrong to stop newspapers publishing the stories they want to.

> **Useful language**
>
> I agree with statement 1.
> So do I. / I don't.
>
> I don't agree with statement 2 because ...
> Nor do I. / I do.

Exposed!

(a) **ARRESTED AGAIN**

(b) **FOUND SAFE AND SOUND**

(c) **DISCOVERED ... NAKED AND DRUNK**

(d) **HOSPITALISED**

(e) **TRAPPED IN ZOO**

(f) **CAUGHT ON CAMERA**

1 The monkey who escaped from Bristol Zoo last weekend was discovered by school children yesterday. Police say that the animal, who was found in a school playground, was fine but a little hungry. The zoo admitted that it needed to improve its security.

2 Hollywood resident Helen Hicks was stopped by police early on Sunday morning after dancing around her neighbourhood with no clothes on. Hicks had drunk half a bottle of vodka after an argument with her rock guitarist boyfriend Johnny Hedges. A friend says that Ms Hicks was suffering from depression.

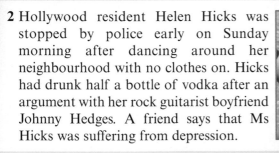

3 Lion tamer Sergei Ivanov was seriously injured by his lion, Sheba, during last night's performance of the Moscow Circus. Ivanov has worked in the circus for over twenty-five years. He was taken to Springfields General Hospital last night. Doctors say that he is lucky to be alive.

4 Super-rich male model Justin Orlando's gay love affair with British pop singer Ross Curtis was exposed this week. The two men were photographed together in a London restaurant. Orlando, who has never tried to hide his sexuality, said that he was very happy with his new partner.

Reading

1 Match the newspaper articles (1–4) with the headlines (a–f). You will not need two of the headlines.

2 Are these statements true or false? If false, explain why.

1 The zoo said they were responsible for the monkey's escape.
2 Helen took her clothes off as a joke.
3 Sergei hadn't had much experience with animals.
4 Justin wanted to hide his sexuality.

Language focus

Past Simple passive

Look at the articles and underline verbs in the Past Simple passive. Are any of the verbs irregular?

Which verb form is used in the headlines?

See Workbook, pp. 52–3, ex 6.

Practice

1 Choose the correct sentence, a) or b).

1 a) The monkey was discovered by school children.
  b) The monkey discovered the school children.
2 a) Helen Hicks was stopped by police.
  b) Helen Hicks stopped the police.
3 a) Sheba was seriously injured by Sergei Ivanov.
  b) Sheba seriously injured Sergei Ivanov.

2 Change these headlines into sentences in the Past Simple passive.

EXAMPLE:
Dog bites owner.
An owner was bitten by his / her dog.
Hunter attacked by bear.
A hunter was attacked by a bear.

1 Gangster shoots mafia boss
2 CIA find drugs in rap group's bags
3 French elect new president
4 Police arrest top model
5 City centre destroyed by fire
6 Celebrities invited to Queen's party

Reading

1 Try to put these events from the Helen Hicks story into the correct order.

a) She went home.
b) She was taken to the police station and charged.
c) Neighbours heard shouting.
d) She spent the night with her rock star boyfriend.
e) She took off her nightdress.
f) She left the house angrily.
g) A Los Angeles police car picked her up.

Read a longer newspaper article about Helen Hicks and check.

2 Match the paragraphs in the article (1–5) with the descriptions (a–e).

a) background information on Helen Hicks
b) how Helen Hicks felt
c) a summary of the news story
d) the end of the story
e) an eye-witness account of what happened

Writing

A news story

Write a newspaper article using one of the stories on page 74. Organise your story in five paragraphs.

Paragraph 1: Summary of news story
Paragraph 2: Background information on main character
Paragraph 3: What happened (eye-witness account)
Paragraph 4: How the story ended
Paragraph 5: How everyone felt in the end

Pronunciation

/h/

1 Look at this sentence. Which of the four *h*s is silent?

What happened to Helen in Hollywood?

(8.5) Listen and repeat.

2 Look at these words. Which *h*s are silent?

alcohol   character   ghost   hangover
headline   honest   hour   hurry
neighbourhood   vehicle   which   whole

(8.6) Listen, check and repeat.

3 Practise saying these tabloid newspaper headlines.

1 Hollywood hotel in hurricane hell
2 Hippy hit for Harriet
3 Honest Harry in hospital again
4 Hangover for hungry horse

(8.7) Listen and check.

HELEN HICKS ARRESTED

Helen Hicks

1 HOLLYWOOD. 36-year-old multi-millionairess divorcee Helen Hicks was arrested early on Sunday morning by Los Angeles police after she had walked around her neighbourhood drunk and completely naked.

2 Helen is the close friend of a number of Hollywood stars. She had spent the night with her rock guitarist boyfriend Johnny Hedges at her home. The house is in Somerset Gardens Paradise, one of the most exclusive neighbourhoods in Hollywood.

3 Neighbours say that at about 1 am they heard people shouting inside the house. Then Ms Hicks ran out of the house wearing only her nightclothes. 'She was really drunk. She couldn't even walk in a straight line,' said neighbour Dorothy Sánchez. 'I saw her walking down the road in a terrible state and then she started taking off her nightdress. I was so embarrassed!'

4 At around 1.45 am, a Los Angeles police car picked up Ms Hicks. She was taken to Mount Pleasant police station where she gave evidence and was charged with indecent exposure. At about 5 am she was allowed to go home.

5 'I had drunk too much and I didn't know what I was doing. I have been very depressed recently,' said Ms Hicks in the morning. She admitted that she had a terrible hangover.

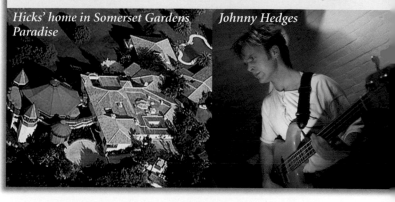

Hicks' home in Somerset Gardens Paradise   *Johnny Hedges*

A good luck story: Try exs 1–3 on your CD-Rom.

You must be joking!

Speaking

Discuss these questions.

1 What is gossip?
2 What do you gossip about?
3 Is gossip always a bad thing?
4 Why do you think gossip is popular?

Reading

1 Do men and women gossip about different things? Read the text and find out what Michael and Sharon think.

2 Answer the questions.

   1 According to Michael, what does Sharon gossip about?
   2 According to Sharon, what does Michael gossip about?
   3 What do they think of gossip? Why?
   4 According to Sharon, why do men say that they don't gossip?

3 Find words or expressions in the text that mean the same as these.

  Michael
   1 finish a relationship
   2 a cheap offer in the shops
   3 hate
   4 type of thing
   5 boring

  Sharon
   6 laugh at
   7 relax

Who's got the gossip?

A new survey of a thousand young people reveals that men gossip just as much as women. Men around the country, however, are quick to say that this isn't true.

Michael Weiner, a 25-year-old builder from Arizona, says:
5 'Women gossip much more than men. My girlfriend Sharon is terrible. She's always gossiping with her friends – who's going out with who, who's split up. If it's not that, it's shopping, clothes, where to find a bargain … Or she gossips about famous people – love affairs and scandals in Hollywood. I can't stand that stuff. Celebrity gossip's really
10 dull. I mean, why are those people so important? When I'm out with my friends, we talk about more important things. We don't waste our time gossiping.'

But women are not surprised about the survey's results. We spoke to Michael's girlfriend, **Sharon Morris**, who tells us: 'Michael says he
15 and his friends don't gossip but they do. Maybe it's not as obvious, but boys do it just the same. They make fun of each other a lot, especially about girls, and about the cars they drive. Men are stupid because they think it's embarrassing to gossip. They think it's just what girls do. But there's nothing wrong with it – it's completely natural, and
20 it's fun, too. It's a really good way to unwind. Sometimes you don't want to think about serious things.'

Michael Weiner and Sharon Morris

Try the internet activities for this unit at www.webframework.net.

Listening

1 🔊 8.8 Listen to four conversations and answer the questions.

1 Match the conversations (1–4) with the pictures (a–d). What are they talking about?

2 What is the speakers' relationship?

> schoolfriends neighbours
> cousins colleagues

2 Listen again. Who uses these expressions? Write the conversation number.

a) She's only got herself to blame. 2
b) It was really funny.
c) It's in really bad taste.
d) Good for her.
e) It's her own fault.
f) I'm dead jealous.
g) It's completely absurd.

3 What do the speakers think of the person they are gossiping about?

TAKEAWAY ENGLISH: *Gossiping*

1 Continue the dialogues (1–5) with a suitable question (a–e).

a) Who to? d) Are you sure?
b) ~~Where were they?~~ e) What was the problem?
c) Who's the mother?

1 A: Did you hear the news? The other day, we saw Tracy kissing Gary.
   B: That's incredible! <u>Where were they?</u>

2 A: Did you know that Harry and June broke up last week?
   B: Are you serious? _____

3 A: Have you heard that Robin's got engaged again?
   B: You must be joking! _____

4 A: Did you know that Brian's got a kid?
   B: No! I don't believe it! _____

5 A: Everyone says that it's over. She wants to leave him.
   B: Really? _____

🔊 8.9 Listen to the dialogues and check your answers.

2 Work in pairs. Continue one of the dialogues to make a gossipy conversation.

EXAMPLE:
A: Did you hear the news? We saw Tracy kissing Gary.
B: That's incredible! Where were they?
A: In the pub, in front of everybody.
B: Really? Who else was there? ...

Useful language

Really?	No! I don't believe it!	You must be joking!
Are you serious?	That's incredible!	

Song

🔊 8.10 *I heard it through the grapevine:* See resource sheet 8B.

9 Hi-tech

- Second conditional
- Reported statements
- Gadgets
- Time verbs
- Machine nouns & verbs
- /aɪ/
- Telephoning – business or pleasure?

Time savers

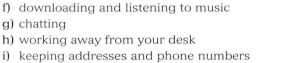

Vocabulary

Gadgets

Match the gadgets (1–10) with their uses (a–j).

1 discman	a) playing electronic games
2 DVD player	b) listening to music
3 games console	c) changing TV channel
4 laptop	d) putting pictures onto a computer
5 CD burner	e) watching films
6 mobile	f) downloading and listening to music
7 palmtop	g) chatting
8 remote control	h) working away from your desk
9 scanner	i) keeping addresses and phone numbers
10 MP3 player	j) recording music CDs and CD-Roms

Which gadgets can you see in the picture? Which ones do you own?

Speaking

How much time do you spend doing these things each week? Is it a waste of time?

1 texting messages on your mobile
2 playing computer games
3 shopping on the internet
4 chatting online
5 watching satellite TV channels
6 answering e-mails
7 surfing the net
8 playing games on your mobile

Listening

 Listen to four teenagers talking about how technology wastes and saves their time. Complete the table.

	Darren	Charlene	Abdul	Cristina
How do they waste time?	chatting online			
How much time do they waste?			½ an hour every day	
How do they save time?				

Vocabulary

Time verbs

Complete the sentences with the correct form of these verbs.

| kill | run out of | save |
| spend | waste | |

1 Going by plane _____ me a lot of time because the train takes eight hours.
2 I didn't do anything last Sunday. I just _____ time, sitting on the sofa and watching telly.
3 My exams start next week so I've got to _____ time studying this weekend.
4 You shouldn't _____ time cleaning. Why don't you employ someone to do it for you?
5 Oh dear, we'll have to stop there. We've just _____ time, I'm afraid.

 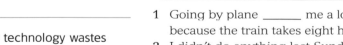 *Time verbs: Try exs 1–4 on your CD-Rom.*

Reading & Speaking

1 What do you think a 'kidult' is?

2 Before you read the article, say whether you think these sentences are true (T) or false (F).

1 British kids get the most pocket money in Europe.
2 Most children in the UK aged between eleven and fourteen have mobile phones.
3 The bedroom is the most important room in the house for Italian kids.
4 Children in the UK spend on average seven hours a day watching TV.
5 Technology is improving young people's reading habits.

Read and check your answers.

3 Match the paragraphs (1–5) with the headings (a–e).

a) Money in their pockets 2
b) Kids are young adults
c) Hooked to the screen
d) Bedroom culture
e) Crazy about technology

4 Discuss these questions.

1 Did you have your own room when you were a child? What about a TV?
2 What are the advantages and / or disadvantages of kids
   a) having a TV in their bedroom?
   b) knowing so much about technology?

KIDULTS
the technology consuming our kids

I They are brother and sister. He buys computer magazines and knows more about palmtops than his father. She can download music from the internet onto her mobile and burn her own CDs. He's thirteen. She's nine. Welcome to the world of kidults, where young children behave as if they were in their twenties.

2 British kids are the most spoilt in Europe. They get on average £13 a week pocket money, twice the rate in Italy. UK parents spend less time with their kids but they spend much more money on them.

3 According to research done by Value Engineers, 70 per cent of young teens in the UK have a mobile phone and 15 per cent have their own computer. And unlike their parents, kidults are not afraid to experiment with technology.

4 Experts say that one reason for this is the many hours that British kids spend in their rooms. If you ask ten year olds in Italy which is the most important room in the house, they'll say the kitchen. The British equivalent will always say his or her own bedroom. The majority of UK teenagers have their own bedroom complete with CD player, while 25 per cent even have their own TV / video and electronic games.

5 On average, UK kids spend an incredible seven hours a day watching the screen – playing games, chatting online or killing time watching TV. As a result, have adolescents forgotten how to read? The answer seems to be yes. Reading requires concentration and technology has killed this.

Mobile madness

Speaking

1 In pairs, answer these questions.

  1 Do you have a mobile phone?

  2 If you have one, how often do you use it? Do
you mostly make calls or send text messages as
well? How much does your mobile cost you
every month?

  3 If you don't have one, would you like to? Why /
Why not?

2 Make a list of the advantages and disadvantages of
mobile phones.

Advantages	Disadvantages
Useful in emergencies	Anti-social

Reading

What kind of relationship do you have with your mobile?
Do the questionnaire then turn to page 122. Do you
agree with the description?

You and your
messages

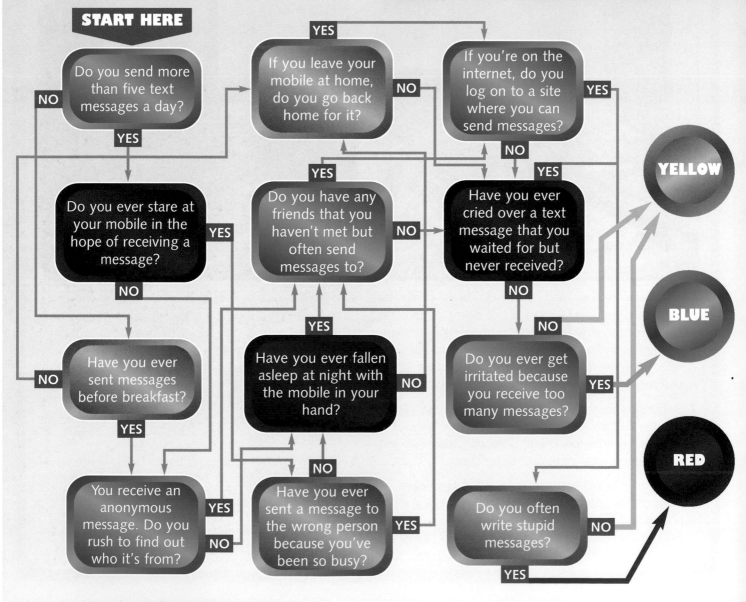

START HERE

Do you send more than five text messages a day? — NO / YES

If you leave your mobile at home, do you go back home for it? — YES / NO

If you're on the internet, do you log on to a site where you can send messages? — YES / NO

Do you ever stare at your mobile in the hope of receiving a message? — YES / NO

Do you have any friends that you haven't met but often send messages to? — YES / NO

Have you ever cried over a text message that you waited for but never received? — YES / NO

Have you ever sent messages before breakfast? — NO / YES

Have you ever fallen asleep at night with the mobile in your hand? — YES / NO

Do you ever get irritated because you receive too many messages? — YES / NO

You receive an anonymous message. Do you rush to find out who it's from? — YES / NO

Have you ever sent a message to the wrong person because you've been so busy? — NO / YES

Do you often write stupid messages? — YES / NO

YELLOW

BLUE

RED

Language focus

Second conditional

> **Look at the examples of the second conditional and complete the rules.**
>
> *If I won the lottery, I'd buy a new computer.*
> *If I didn't have a games console, I wouldn't waste so much time.*
>
> To form the second conditional, we use:
> *If +* ...., *would + infinitive.*
> The contracted form of *would* is ....
> The negative form of *would* is ....
>
> **Note:** Sometimes we use *were* instead of *was* in second conditional sentences.
> *If I were you, I'd get a new mobile.*
>
> **Which situation is more probable? Look at the examples and complete the rules below.**
>
> **First conditional**
>
> *If he loses his mobile, he will be really upset.* (He is always losing things.)
>
> **Second conditional**
>
> *If she lost her mobile tomorrow, she would be really upset.* (She's usually careful with it.)
>
> We use the .... conditional to express a future possibility and its consequence.
>
> We use the .... conditional to express situations which are improbable, impossible or imaginary in the present or future.
>
> **Translate the two examples above into your language. Do you form them in the same way?**
>
> ....
> ....
>
> *See Reference Guide, p.14.*
> *See Workbook, pp. 57–8, exs 1–5.*

Practice

1 Do you think these things are probable (P) or improbable (I) in your life? Make a first or second conditional sentence for each one.

1 my computer breaks down
   I – If my computer broke down, I would lose all my work.
2 lose my mobile
3 appear on television
4 do an online English course
5 go to the gym every day
6 be sunny tomorrow
7 fail my exams
8 get a new job

2 Match the columns to make sentences in the second conditional.

1 If I had more time,
2 If I did more sport,
3 If I didn't have a television,
4 If I had a better car,
5 If I earned more money,
6 If I didn't work / study,

a) I wouldn't know what to do.
b) I would study more English.
c) I would go on holiday to Australia.
d) I would drive a lot faster.
e) I wouldn't waste so much time.
f) I would feel a lot fitter.

3 Complete the sentences in the left-hand column of exercise 2 so that they are true for you.

EXAMPLE: *If I had more time, I would go to the cinema more often.*

Pronunciation

'd and *'ll*

1 (9.2) Listen to these conditional sentences. In which do you hear *'d* and in which do you hear *'ll*?

2 Turn to Reference Guide, page 55, and look at transcript 9.2. Practise saying the sentences with short forms.

Listening

1 (9.3) Listen and match the mobile phone conversations (1–4) with the pictures (a–d).

2 Listen again. Write down a possible reply for each of the twelve silences.

3 (9.4) Listen to the whole conversations. How many of your replies were similar?

Chat rooms

Speaking & Listening

1 Discuss these questions.

   1 Do you use e-mail or the internet?

   2 If you do, how often do you log on? How long do you spend online?

   3 If you don't, would you like to? Why / Why not?

2 Make a list of the uses of the internet.

   You can use it to ...

3 Look at the homepages of two websites and answer the questions.

   1 If you wanted to read the news online, which website would you prefer? Why?

   2 Do you prefer to read the news in the newspaper or online? What's the difference?

4 (9.5) Listen to Nat talking about one of the websites. Answer the questions.

   1 Which one does he prefer? Why?

   2 What is his favourite section?

   3 What other features does he mention?

   4 Does he still buy a daily newspaper?

5 Work in pairs. Ask and answer about your favourite website.

   1 How often do you log on to it?

   2 What features does it include?

   3 Why would you recommend it?

Try the internet activities for this unit at www.webframework.net.

Reading & Listening

1 What is a chat room? Have you ever chatted with strangers on the internet?

2 Read this chat room conversation and answer the questions.

   1 Do the two people know each other well?

   2 Have they met before?

   3 What do you think will happen on their date?

Cute Chick 24> So, shall we meet up and have a drink?

Boy Next Door> GR8. When is good for you?

Cute Chick 24> What are you doing at the weekend?

Boy Next Door> On Sunday, nothing.

Cute Chick 24> Let's eat out.

Boy Next Door> It will be wonderful to find out what you look like at last.

Cute Chick 24> I can't wait.

Boy Next Door> I'll take you to a great place I know, very smart. ;)

Cute Chick 24> GR8.

Boy Next Door> And I've bought you something special as well! :)

Cute Chick 24> Oh, wow! :)

3  Listen to Cute Chick 24 telling a friend about her date with Boy Next Door. Answer the questions.

   1 Did the date go well?

   2 What lies had he told her?

   3 What did they do on the date?

   4 What happened in the end?

   5 What does she think about chat rooms now?

Speaking

What do you think of chat rooms? Why do you think they are so popular? What are the dangers of making friends this way?

Language focus
Reported statements

9.7 Listen and complete the reported statements.

Direct statement		Reported statement
I **am** tall and handsome.	→	1 He told me that he was tall and handsome.
I **am living** in a fantastic flat.	→	2 He said he .... in a fantastic flat.
I **will take** you to a smart restaurant.	→	3 He said that he .... me to a smart restaurant.
I **have bought** you a special present.	→	4 He told me he .... me a special present.
I **studied** at Oxford.	→	5 He said he .... at Oxford.

Complete the rules for the tense changes.

Direct statement		Reported statement
Present Simple	→	Past Simple
....	→	Past Continuous
will + infinitive	→	....
....	→	was / were going to
Present Perfect	→	....
....	→	Past Perfect (or Past Simple)

Note: We can use *told* + object or *said* (with no object) to introduce a reported statement.

Sometimes we use *that* to introduce a reported statement, but it isn't necessary.

See Reference Guide, p.14. See Workbook, pp. 58–9, exs 6–8.

Practice

Rewrite these direct statements as reported statements.

1 You are really sexy. (He said) He said that I was really sexy.
2 We'll be at the restaurant at 9 pm. (We told her)
3 I've sent him lots of e-mails but I haven't met him. (She said)
4 We went home straight after the meal. (She told me)
5 In the summer I'm going to study English in Seattle. (He said)
6 They are really excited about their date. (She said)

The Real Thing: *No way!*

1 Look at Cute Chick 24's final comment. Underline the correct word in sentences 1–2 below.

I'll never go back into a chat room again in my life! No way!

   1 She's sure that she **will** / **won't** go back.

   2 *No way!* is a **formal** / **informal** expression.

2 Write down possible responses to these lines of dialogue, using *No way!*

EXAMPLE: Is it easy to learn to drive?
   No way! I found it really difficult.

   1 Do you think the Green Party will win the election?

   2 Do you want to work late tonight?

   3 David Beckham is the world's best footballer.

   4 Are you going shopping on Saturday?

9.8 Listen and compare. Which word is stressed in *No way!*

Communication breakdown

Listening

1 What can go wrong with the following equipment?

> alarm clock   laptop   microwave
> photocopier   video recorder

2 🔊(9.9) Listen to four people talking about the problems they have had. What equipment are they talking about?

3 Listen again. What was the problem? What was the consequence of the problem?

Vocabulary
Machine nouns and verbs

1 Match the pictures (a–e) with the nouns (1–5). Then match them with the verbs (i–viii). There are lots of matches for some words.

1	button	i	come on
2	light	ii	go off
3	plug	iii	plug in
4	switch	iv	unplug
5	machine	v	press
		vi	turn / switch on
		vii	turn / switch off
		viii	warm up

How do you say these phrasal verbs in your language?

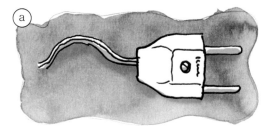

2 Complete the sentences with verbs from exercise 1.

1 There's nothing interesting on TV. Let's <u>switch</u> it <u>off</u>.
2 When the scanner is ready, a red light _____.
3 The photocopier takes a long time to _____.
4 First of all, you have to _____ the green button.
5 If the machine isn't working, check that you have _____ it _____ properly.
6 I want to listen to some music. Can you _____ the radio for me?
7 If the light _____, there's no more power so you have to recharge the battery.
8 The children watch too many videos! I'm going to _____ the video recorder and hide it somewhere while they're asleep.

3 Look at the sentences in exercise 2. Which verbs don't have an object?

4 Which of these sentences is incorrect? Why?

1 You have to turn on the machine.
2 You have to turn the machine on.
3 You have to turn on it.
4 You have to turn it on.

Writing
Giving instructions

Think of a machine or gadget. Write instructions for using it and give them to your partner. Can your partner guess what it is?

EXAMPLE: First you plug it in. You turn it on and clean the floor with it. Then you unplug it again. (A hoover)

Pronunciation
/aɪ/

Mark the stress on these words. Which word is different?

mobile   missile   meanwhile   fragile   aisle   denial   crocodile   Anglophile

🔊(9.10) Listen and check the pronunciation and stress. Which letters are silent?

The telephone: Try exs 1–6 on your CD-Rom.

TAKEAWAY ENGLISH: *Telephoning – business or pleasure?*

1 (9.11) Listen to three telephone conversations and answer the questions.

1 Who is calling on business? Who wants to speak to a friend?
2 What do the three conversations have in common?
3 Which caller: a) speaks to the switchboard?
b) leaves his name?
c) gets a mobile number?

2 Listen to each phone conversation again. In which conversation do you hear these expressions? Write 1, 2 or 3.

The caller
a) Could you tell him that Nick rang? 1
b) It's Denise Forrest here.
c) I'll try again later.
d) I'd like to speak to Mandy Stephenson, please.

The person who receives the call
e) Sorry, he's not in at the moment.
f) Can I take a message?
g) How can I help you?
h) Just one moment, please.
i) I'm afraid he's engaged.
j) Hold the line, please, and I'll put you through.
k) Hang on a sec. I'll just get a pen.
l) Can I ask who's calling?

3 Work in pairs. Look at the prompts and decide what to say. Then have the conversations.

<u>Business phone conversation</u>

Student A	Student B (Caller)
Human Resources	
help you?	speak / Chris Leavy?
ask / who / calling?	name
hold / line / please	
put / through	thanks
sorry / engaged	
leave / message?	no / try again
thanks	thanks / goodbye
goodbye	

<u>Social phone conversation</u>

Student A	Student B (Caller)
hello	speak / Paul?
who?	name
hang / sec	OK
sorry / not in	OK / ring back
leave / message?	tell / called
OK	thanks / bye
bye	

 *Now do Unit test 9 on your CD-Rom.* **85**

Retail therapy

Vox pops

[14:07-15:39] Watch the vox pops and answer the on-screen questions.

1 Watch again. Who says it?

1 I hate shopping.
2 Like all women, I love to shop.
3 I normally spend my money on clothes, music and eating out.

2 Test your memory. Complete the gaps.

JULIETA: I _____ _____ a house if I had more money.

IQBAL: If I had more money, I would buy a _____ house.

JULIETA: I buy _____ _____ _____ in Spain.

OLIVER: Julieta buys my clothes _____ _____ in Spain.

IQBAL: I buy my clothes from _____.

Watch again and check your answers.

Before you watch

1 Discuss in pairs.

1 Do you like shopping?
2 What do you spend your money on?
3 How many designer labels can you think of?

2 Here are two popular places to shop in London. What's the difference between them? What can you buy in each place?

Bond Street, London

Camden Market, London

Tracey

While you watch

Sequence 1 [15:40-17:05]

Tracey is an actress. She comes from Canada. She lives in London and she loves shopping!

Watch the sequence and answer the questions.

1 Work in pairs. Are these statements true (T) or false (F)? If false, explain why.

1 Tracey is from the United States. F – She's from Canada.
2 Tracey has lived in London for eight years.
3 Tracey's husband is from England.
4 The only problem with London is that it is expensive.
5 Tracey particularly likes the cinema in London.
6 Tracey doesn't run her own business.

2 Watch the sequence again. Tick the adjectives that you hear.

amazing   beautiful   buzzy   exciting   exhilarating
fantastic   fun   great   incredible✓   rewarding
satisfying   terrible   unbelievable   wonderful

Which adjectives refer to a) London, b) the theatre and c) both?
EXAMPLE: incredible – London

Sequence 2 [17:06-19:27]

Watch the sequence and answer the questions.

1 Who says it – Tracey or the shop assistant?

1 Can I help you at all? shop assistant
2 Oh, I don't know … medium-ish.
3 Well, this is quite nice, isn't it?
4 Do you like the length? Do you like the collar?
5 I quite like this. How much is this one?
6 How do you pay? Cash or card?
7 OK, I'll take it!

2 Test your memory.

1 How many coats do you see in the sequence?
2 How much does Tracey's coat cost?
3 How does she pay for it?

Sequence 3 [19:28-21:02]

Watch the sequence and answer the questions.

1 Tick the adjectives which Tracey uses to describe her taste in clothes.

> casual ✓   designer   elegant   formal
> informal   second-hand   smart   stylish

2 Which item of clothing does she think people should wear more?

a) hats   **b)** jeans

3 What does she buy in Camden market?

a) a white jacket   **b)** a white shirt

4 Why does she like shopping in markets?

a) It's very cheap.

b) There's a great variety of clothing.

Sequence 4 [21:03-22:38]

Watch the sequence and answer the questions.

1 What can Tracey buy in London? Tick the things you hear.

> bags   jewellery   leather goods   shoes
> trousers   umbrellas   wallets   watches

2 What are the differences between shopping in London and Canada? Circle the correct answer.

1 London is **more expensive / cheaper** than Canada.

2 Shopping in Canada is **not as exciting / as exciting** as shopping in London.

3 The inside of shops in Canada are **older / newer** than in London.

3 Which is Tracey's favourite department store?

a) Selfridges   **b)** Harrods   **c)** Fenwicks

Watch the whole DVD again and answer the on-screen questions.

After you watch

Can you remember? Work in pairs. What clothes do we see Tracey wearing during the programme?

World culture:
Global fashion

1 Nowadays, designer labels are everywhere – Nike ... Ralph Lauren ... Lacoste! How many of these fashion labels can you identify?

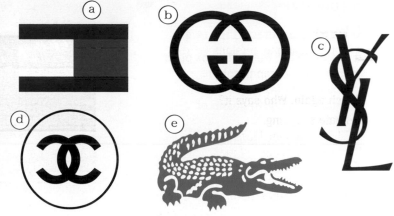

2 Match the fashion labels with their countries of origin on the map. (Some of the labels come from the same country.)

> Burberry   Hugo Boss   Camper   Dolce and Gabanna
> Tommy Hilfiger   Donna Karan (DKNY)   Lacoste

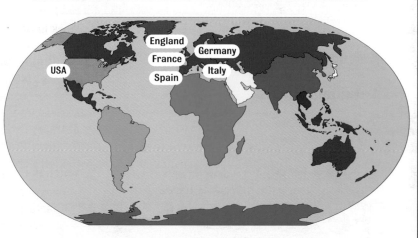

3 Work in pairs. Discuss these questions about fashion in your country.

1 Which fashion designers do you know in your country?

2 Which countries do your clothes come from?

3 Which country's fashions do you like the most?

4 Answer the questions with the correct fashion designer.

> Calvin Klein   Gianni Versace   Carolina Herrera   Ralph Lauren

Who ...

1 ... started their career making ties?

2 ... was shot in 1997?

3 ... is well-known for underwear?

4 ... used controversial adverts?

5 ... is famous for women's clothes?

6 ... has a perfume called 202?

Flashback 3

Vocabulary

1 a Match the extracts (1–6) with the newspaper sections (a–c).

b Classify the important vocabulary from Exercise 1a into a) money, b) gossip or c) technology.

EXAMPLE: c) mobile phone

c In pairs, write more words and expressions in the boxes.

Look at Units 7–9 and check your answers.

Writing & Speaking

1 a Work in pairs. Turn to page 124.

b (F3.1) Listen to the phone conversations. Compare them with your versions.

c Roleplay your conversations.

Language focus

1 Write the news story from the notes. Use the correct form of the underlined verbs in the active or passive.

a Money   **b** Gossip   **c** Technology

① … a government study reports that mobile phones don't represent a health risk …

② … most people can't afford to save and have to borrow cash to buy a new car …

③ … the majority of people have a laptop but, in the future, most people will probably use a palmtop …

④ … make sure it's plugged in. Then switch it on and you'll see a red light …

⑤ … confirming the rumour that the 23-year-old celebrity is spending time at a Los Angeles drug rehabilitation centre …

⑥ … waiters don't earn a big salary but most people leave a tip …

Text message saves man's life

A climber was rescued yesterday after a text message helped a helicopter to find him.

Don Cleese, 38 …

Climber <u>rescue</u> yesterday after text message <u>help</u> helicopter to find him.

Don Cleese, 38, <u>climb</u> in Snowdonia when he <u>fall</u> and <u>break</u> a leg.

He <u>use</u> his phone to make 999 emergency call and rescue helicopter <u>sent</u> to look for him.

Helicopter <u>can't</u> find climber and pilot <u>decide</u> to send text message. Mr Cleese <u>receive</u> message and <u>phone</u> helicopter. Pilot <u>use</u> call to locate him.

Mr Cleese <u>take</u> to hospital in Bangor but he <u>send</u> home early this morning.

'I <u>give</u> phone as a Christmas present,' he said. 'It's the best present I ever <u>have</u>'.

2 a Complete the quiz with *will* or *would*.

Do you love the world of gossip?

1 If there's a programme on TV tonight about the private lives of famous people, _____ you …
   a) watch it?
   b) change to a different channel?
   c) have it on in the background

2 If you won the lottery, _____ you …
   a) tell your story to all the newspapers?
   b) keep it secret?
   c) tell only your family and friends?

3 If you could meet anyone in the world, _____ you …
   a) meet a popular star?
   b) meet a politician?
   c) meet someone you've admired for a long time?

4 If a colleague is gossiping in your office tomorrow, _____ you …
   a) pay full attention.
   b) ignore him / her.
   c) pretend not to listen.

5 If a famous sports / music personality comes to your town in the near future, _____ you …
   a) wait for hours to see them?
   b) read about it in the newspaper the next day?
   c) go to see them if your friends want to?

6 You _____ go to a TV studio if …
   a) all your friends could see you.
   b) there was a serious debate.
   c) it was a show you really liked.

b In pairs, ask and answer the questions. Turn to the answer key on page 124. Do you agree?

3 Complete the gossip column using the interview notes.

Chit chat

Lilita was in town this week on tour. After the gig I spoke to her.

I asked her if she was very tired but she said that she was very happy with the tour and that everything …

When I asked her if she'd had time to see London, she said …

We all want to know if there's any truth in the rumours about her marriage. She said …

1) This is the third month of the tour. Are you very tired?

'I'm very happy with the tour. Everything's going well. We started the tour eight weeks ago and the public has been fantastic.'

2) Have you had time to see London?

'Well, I got up very late and haven't had time to go out. But I'll be back later in the year and I'll spend a bit more time here.'

3) Is it true that you've split up with your husband?

'Everything's fine between us. We've decided to spend some time apart for artistic reasons.'

You *choose!*

Put together a class magazine. Work in groups and choose one of the article ideas below.

1 Write an article about how technology, e.g. a mobile phone, saved someone's life.

OR

2 Write a questionnaire asking what your classmates will / would do in different situations.

OR

3 Interview a famous person.
   a Work in two groups. Choose a famous person and write questions.
   b Work with someone from the other group. Roleplay the interview, then swap roles.
   c Write a report of your interview.

Put all the articles together, and read your magazine!

- Adverbs
- Relative pronouns: *who, which, that, where*
- Foreign words
- /t ʃ/ & /k/
- Class language

Culture shock

Speaking

Discuss these questions.

1 Would you like to live in a foreign country? Where and for how long?
2 If you did, would you try to learn the language immediately?
3 Would you try to mix with the locals or socialise with other ex-pats?
4 Can you think of any foreign places where a lot of British or American people live?

Listening

1 🎧(10.1) Listen and match the ex-pats, Dean, Carl, Marina and Ellen, with the cities (a–d) and the jobs (i–iv).

   i lawyer   ii tour guide   iii taxi driver   iv English teacher

2 Listen again and answer true (T) or false (F). If false, explain why.

1 Dean can't understand his clients. F
2 His sister Trisha speaks perfect Spanish.
3 Carl uses Chinese in his job.
4 He feels very integrated now.
5 Marina is trying hard to improve her Arabic.
6 She would like a new job.
7 Ellen didn't like living in Japan when she couldn't speak the language.
8 She speaks to her Japanese boyfriend's friends and family in English.

Dean

Carl

Marina

Ellen

3 (10.2) Listen to Trisha, Carl, Marina and Ellen discussing strategies for language learning. Match the speakers with the techniques in the pictures (a–d).

4 Listen again and answer the questions.

1 Which speakers talk about the following? What do they say about them?
   a) vocabulary
   b) speaking
   c) colloquial expressions
   d) technical terms
   e) reading
   f) following a conversation
   g) making mistakes

2 Who is happy with his / her progress? Who is unhappy? Why?

5 Do you think these are good or bad strategies for learning English? Why?

6 (10.3) Listen and complete the sentences with the adverbs you hear.

1 I'm _____ making mistakes.
2 I can _____ learn 50 words every week.
3 I read very _____.
4 Now I can speak quite _____.
5 I can talk _____ in Japanese now.

Language focus

Adverbs

Turn to Reference Guide, page 58, and look at transcript 10.2. Classify the adverbs in bold into these types.

1 manner   fluently, ...   2 frequency   always, ...

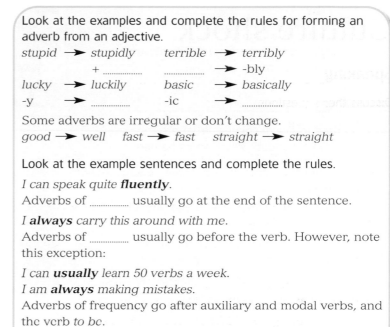

Look at the examples and complete the rules for forming an adverb from an adjective.

stupid	→ stupidly	terrible	→ terribly
	+	....	→ -bly
lucky	→ luckily	basic	→ basically
-y	→	-ic	→ ....

Some adverbs are irregular or don't change.

good → well   fast → fast   straight → straight

Look at the example sentences and complete the rules.

*I can speak quite **fluently**.*
Adverbs of .... usually go at the end of the sentence.

*I **always** carry this around with me.*
Adverbs of .... usually go before the verb. However, note this exception:

*I can **usually** learn 50 verbs a week.*
*I am **always** making mistakes.*
Adverbs of frequency go after auxiliary and modal verbs, and the verb *to be*.

See Reference Guide, p.15.
See Workbook, pp. 66–7, exs 1–4.

Practice

Make adverbs from these adjectives.

EXAMPLE: automatically

~~automatic~~   bad   brilliant   careful   fantastic   fast
good   gradual   happy   incredible   lazy   normal
recent   sad   serious   straight   strange   terrible

Pronunciation

/tʃ/ and /k/

1 (10.4) Listen and complete the sentences.

1 _____, I'm able to travel a lot.
2 _____, I missed the bus.
3 He arrived very _____.
4 _____ they left the party.

2 Listen again and mark the stress on the adverbs. What sounds do these words have in common?

3 (10.5) Underline the /tʃ/ sounds that you hear.

chaos   character   chatting   chemist   chocolate
choose   headache   match   research   rich

Which words don't have a /tʃ/ sound? How else is *ch* sometimes pronounced?

4 (10.6) Listen and repeat these words with /tʃ/.

adventure   catch   chicken   child   furniture   future
kitchen   picture   switch   unfortunately   culture

Adverbs of frequency: Try exs 1–2 on your CD-Rom.   **91**

Small talk

Speaking

Answer the questions.

1 What is small talk?
2 What do you say to each other before and after the class starts?
3 What topics do people usually talk about when there is nothing else to say?

Listening

1 (10.7) Listen to five dialogues. What are the people talking about? What words helped you decide?

2 (10.8) Listen to the rest of the last dialogue. Compare with the diary version and answer the questions.

   1 Which words were used in the spoken version but not in the diary version?
   2 Did you notice any other differences?

Spoken version   Diary version
this Mexican place   a Mexican restaurant

May

Saturday 19th

First we went out for a drink at a cocktail bar that Jane knew. It was really nice there, although the drinks were very expensive. Then we went to a Mexican restaurant for supper. I had a spicy chicken dish with salad and Jane had tacos and we both had margaritas of course. Then we went to a club and danced until six in the morning. I woke up the next morning feeling really bad. I didn't want to do anything the whole day.

The Real Thing: *sort of / kind of / like*

1 (10.9) Listen and match the speakers (1–4) with the pictures (a–d). Do we use *sort of*, *kind of* and *like* to make something more or less specific?

2 (10.10) Listen to someone describing his weekend and make notes. Listen again and write a diary entry for the weekend.

Saturday 26th September
I went to a campsite with some friends in the mountains ...

3 Listen again. How many times does the man say *like* and *sort of*? Turn to Reference Guide, page 59, and check in transcript 10.10.

Vocabulary

Foreign words

1 Which of these English words are used in your language? Are the words used in the same way in English?

cool	fashion	feeling	internet	look	OK
party	sandwich	show	walkman	weekend	

2 These words are used in English but come from other languages. What do the words mean?

algebra	au pair	bungalow	chic
macho	sauna	shampoo	siesta

Check your answers in a dictionary.

3 (10.11) Mark the stress on the words in exercise 2 and guess which language they come from. Then listen and check.

Try the internet activities for this unit at www.webframework.net.

Reading & Speaking

1 Read this article on Spanglish in New York. Which is the best title?

   a) Spanglish – a dead language
   b) A history of Spanglish
   c) Spanglish invades New York
   d) Spanglish – in defence of a new language

2 Are these sentences true (T) or false (F)? If false, explain why.

   1 The Spanish-speaking population has grown very fast recently. T
   2 More people are interested in studying Spanish than before.
   3 Spanglish is mainly used in formal contexts.
   4 Norma Rodriguez doesn't notice when she is speaking Spanglish.
   5 Juan Cortés is against Spanglish because he feels stupid speaking it.
   6 Most academics are against Spanglish because they see it as vulgar.

3 Test your partner. What do these numbers in the text refer to?

   1 1.2 million   3 400,000
   2 1 in 5   4 3rd

4 Discuss these questions.

   1 Are you in favour or against hybrid languages such as Spanglish or Franglais?

   2 Are there any regions in your country where two languages are spoken? Do the two languages get confused?

SPANGLISH

In which city can you read signs like 'Aparca your car aquí' or 'Cuidado con los pickpockets'? **Travelguide** investigates.

1.2 million Hispanics live in the Big Apple and one in five New Yorkers speaks Spanish at home. In the last ten years, the Hispanic population has grown by 400,000. The whole city is learning Spanish like crazy, from businessmen to schoolchildren.

There is a new language, SPANGLISH – a strange mixture of Spanish and English – which is invading the city. The *New York Times* recently said that it had become the city's third official language. Its use is colloquial and often limited to short sentences and signs. Many New Yorkers now wear *socketines* on their feet, drop something on the *carpeta*, shop for *grocerias* and have *cornfley* ('cornflakes') for breakfast.

Norma Rodríguez, a 45-year-old Cuban living in Washington Heights, says it forms a part of her life now: 'Sometimes, you don't realize that you're mixing the two languages. You just hear them both all the time and find that you're inventing new words.' Other people, however, are fighting against this new street language. Businessman Juan Cortés sees it as a sign that the Spanish language is being destroyed. 'It's difficult, but I try not to speak it – it feels vulgar to me.'

Meanwhile, a surprising number of academics have spoken in favour of Spanglish. José María Ruiz, from NY State University, even runs courses in Spanglish and has written a dictionary. 'It is a dialogue between two languages and cultures. We have to accept that languages change and evolve. The only languages that never change are dead ones.'

José María Ruiz   Norma Rodríguez   Juan Cortés

Gaelic in crisis: Try exs 1–2 on your CD-Rom.   **93**

World lingo

Listening

🎧 Listen to five people speaking in different languages and answer the questions.

1 Can you guess which languages they are speaking?
2 Each person is saying the same thing in their language. What are they saying?
3 Which languages do you think sound attractive? Which sound unattractive?

Speaking & Reading

1 Discuss these questions.

1 How many languages are spoken in your country?
2 Are the minority languages in your country becoming more or less popular?
3 Do you think all these languages will still exist in 200 years?

2 In pairs, answer the questions. Choose from these languages.

> Chinese   English   Hindi   Spanish   Yiddish

1 Which is the third most spoken language, with 250 million speakers?
2 Which language is spoken by 4.5 million people but belongs to no country?
3 Which language is spoken by the greatest number of people as a first language?
4 Which language is one of 950 languages and dialects spoken in one country?
5 Which language has grown 50 per cent in the last 50 years?

Now read the text and check your answers.

Languages in Danger!

Over 50 per cent of the world's 5000 languages will be extinct by the end of the next century, according to a recent study. One cause of this is the invasion of territories in which indigenous people live; another is mass migration; a third is the advantage gained by speaking one of the world's most popular languages – Chinese (the language with the greatest number of native speakers), Spanish (with over a quarter of a billion speakers), Hindi and, of course, English.

Knowledge of English has increased around 50 per cent in the last 50 years. There are now an incredible 700 million speakers. It is used as an official language in 60 countries and is now spoken by more people as a second language (over 350 million) than as a first. Against this monster, there is little that minority languages can do.

DID YOU KNOW?

• California is the most linguistically diverse region of the United States with 50 native American languages. However, in recent times a Californian language has died out approximately once a year.

• Hindi is one of 950 languages and dialects in India, some of which are in danger of extinction.

• The number of Indian languages in Brazil has dropped from 1000 to 200 in the last two centuries.

• The world's most endangered language is Alaska's Eyak, which has just one remaining speaker.

• Yiddish, a mixture of German and Hebrew, belongs to no particular country. The number of Yiddish speakers is slowly falling, although 4.5 million people still speak it, mainly in London, New York and Israel.

• Dead languages can be brought back to life. Cornish was once spoken in the southwest of England but its only remaining speaker, Dolly Pentreath, died in 1778. Using old documents, the language was revived and there are now 2000 people who speak it.

1.2 billion people now speak Chinese as their first language.

Native American languages are dying out fast.

3 Cover the text and complete the gaps. Use *who*, *which* or *where*.

1 Name a language <u>which</u> is spoken by more than 700 million people.
2 Name a language _____ is spoken by only one person.
3 Name the last person _____ spoke Cornish before it was revived in the 20th century.
4 Name a country _____ a lot of languages have become extinct in the last 200 years.
5 Name a part of the USA _____ more than 50 languages are spoken.
6 Name a language _____ is a mixture of German and Hebrew.

Now test your partner. How many answers can he / she remember?

Chinese speakers

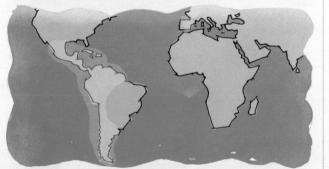

Spanish speakers

Hindi speakers

English speakers

Language focus

Relative pronouns: *who, which, that, where*

Look at the examples and complete the rules.

*I've met a lot of people **who** speak Spanish.*
*There are now a few people **that** speak Cornish.*
We use .... or .... in a relative clause to talk about **people**.

*English is a language **which** is spoken by millions of people.*
*Yiddish and Hebrew are languages **that** are spoken in Israel.*
We use .... or .... in a relative clause to talk about **things**.

*The country **where** they speak most languages is India.*
We use .... in a relative clause to talk about **places**.

Remember that we use *who / that / which* to replace *he / she / they / it*, etc.
Do you know the language which ~~it~~ is spoken by most people?

See Reference Guide, p.15.
See Workbook, pp. 67–8, exs 5–8.

Practice

Complete the sentences with *who, that, which* or *where*.

1 New York is a city <u>where</u> lots of people speak Spanish.
2 Gaelic is a language _____ is dying out.
3 People _____ are bilingual are very lucky.
4 German is the language _____ I want to learn right now.
5 The Basque country is a place _____ many people speak two languages.
6 The thing _____ I find most difficult in English is the pronunciation.

Writing & Speaking

In pairs, write a quiz with ten questions. Use relative clauses.

EXAMPLE: Name the director who made the Star Wars films.
Name the city where you can visit Tiananmen Square.

Swap partners and ask your new partner the questions. How many can he / she answer correctly?

In and out of class

Speaking

Which of these ways of learning a language have you tried?
Which do you think is the best / worst way to learn?

1 going to classes once a week
2 doing an online course
3 going to an English-speaking country for a month
4 going out with an English-speaking person
5 studying at home with special books and / or cassettes
6 listening to songs and watching TV in English

Reading

Read the advert and answer the questions.

1 What is the advert for?
2 What can you achieve in six months?
3 What are the advantages of the system?
4 What special offer is available?
5 What kind of person is the advert trying to attract?

SPEAK QUICK

THE FIRST TOTALLY INTERACTIVE LANGUAGE COURSE!

- Have you tried to learn a foreign language and always failed?
- Do you feel inferior to your colleagues?
- Do you want to learn quickly and in the comfort of your own home?
- Do you want an authentic Speak Quick certificate which will make all your friends jealous?

We guarantee you will be able to have a simple conversation in any language in 6 months ... and that's not all! If you send off today, you can take advantage of this special promotional offer:

BUY ALL 6 CDS FOR THE PRICE OF 5 - *Yes! The complete course for just* €480.

I month trial with no obligation!

PHONE 0900 123 456

Just phone or complete the information below with the language of your choice.

20 languages available:

ARABIC	ICELANDIC
CHINESE	ITALIAN
DANISH	JAPANESE
DUTCH	KOREAN
ENGLISH	NORWEGIAN
FRENCH	POLISH
GERMAN	PORTUGUESE
GREEK	RUSSIAN
HEBREW	THAI
HINDI	TURKISH

Asking about English: Try exs 1–3 on your CD-Rom.

Listening

1 🔊 *10.13* Listen to three people trying to persuade a friend to learn a language. Answer the questions.

1 Which of these languages are they talking about?

> Arabic   French   Japanese
> Portuguese   Russian   Spanish

2 Why do they recommend it?

3 Do they convince their friend?

2 Which of the languages in the list would you prefer to learn? Why?

Speaking

1 Work in groups. Number these in order of importance (1 = most important, 5 = least important) for teachers and students.

THE TEACHER SHOULD:

a) always give us homework.

b) speak in English, never in our language.

c) always correct our mistakes.

d) follow the coursebook as much as possible.

e) try to give us regular tests.

WE SHOULD:

a) only speak English in class.

b) revise each lesson before the next.

c) ask as many questions as possible.

d) only speak in class when we know we're not going to make a mistake.

e) give ourselves learning targets.

Ask another group their opinion. Can you all agree on the one most important thing?

2 Look at the photos. Which type of class do you prefer?

TAKEAWAY ENGLISH: *Class language*

1 🔊 *10.14* Listen to six short dialogues. What does each student want?

2 Listen again and complete.

1 A: _____ I leave twenty minutes early today?
   B: Yes, OK.

2 A: Sorry, _____ I open the window?
   B: Of course you can …

3 A: _____, please? I couldn't hear too well.
   B: Fine. I was explaining how …

4 A: _____ what we have to revise for the exam?
   B: Of course …

5 A: _____ for us, please?
   B: No problem …

6 A: _____ we write in pencil?
   B: It would be better in pen if you have one.

3 🔊 *10.15* Listen and repeat.

1 Is it OK if we finish the class early?

2 Could you repeat that one more time, please?

3 Do you mind if I hand in my work tomorrow?

4 Can you say it more slowly, please?

5 Does it matter if I arrive five minutes late?

6 Could you let us know the marks, please?

4 Work in pairs. Take turns to ask and answer, using these prompts.

1 I / borrow your pen / please

2 you / play the recording again

3 I / use a dictionary / please

4 I / write with a red pen

5 you / ask the question again

6 you / write it on the blackboard / please

11 Street styles

- *-ing* form & infinitive
- Adjective order
- Clothes nouns and adjectives
- Street styles
- /ʃ/ & /ʒ/
- Clothes shopping

Your look

Vocabulary

Clothes adjectives

1 Look at the photos and describe each look. Which do you find most attractive? Why?

2 Match the opposites.

1	formal	a)	smart
2	casual	b)	unfashionable
3	trendy	c)	tight
4	tidy	d)	informal
5	baggy	e)	scruffy

Reading & Speaking

1 Match Matt, Alice, Lucy and Edward with texts 1–4.

2 Describe yourself and people you know. Use the adjectives above.

EXAMPLE: My cousin always looks smart. He wears a suit and tie every day.

3 Look at the four photos again. What type of people do you think they are? Can you tell somebody's character from their 'look'?

Matt   Alice   Lucy

Edward

1 I'm into wearing casual clothes, nothing too formal. I like baggy jeans and trainers and any kind of sporty thing on top – mainly t-shirts and sweatshirts, stuff like that. I don't feel comfortable in smart clothes. I haven't worn a jacket and tie in years. I hate that look – it's so false.

2 I have a wardrobe full of designer labels. I love the American ones particularly – I just adore Calvin Klein and Donna Karan stuff. I think it's worth spending a bit more and getting quality clothes that are going to last. I enjoy looking trendy and wearing the latest fashions. Most people wear such boring clothes. I can't stand that.

3 I prefer wearing scruffy clothes, like old jeans. I haven't bought any new clothes in ages. I can't stand fashion labels. Buying clothes from second-hand shops and markets is fun, and sometimes you can find real bargains.

4 Looking after my appearance is really important. I try to look smart because it makes me feel better about myself. I shave every day and put on a nice, ironed shirt. It's simple: wearing good clothes gives me confidence. Dressing up for special occasions is really good fun as well.

Pronunciation

/ʃ/ *fashion* and /ʒ/ *casual*

1 ◀11.1▶ Listen to these words. Can you hear the difference in pronunciation of the underlined letters?

fa<u>sh</u>ion /ʃ/   ca<u>s</u>ual /ʒ/

2 ◀11.2▶ Listen and tick (✓) the words with a /ʃ/ sound.

occasion   option✓   passion   pleasure
special   sweatshirt   television   treasure

Language focus

-ing form

Find verbs or expressions in the texts on page 98 that mean the same as *I like / dislike*.

like: I love, _____, _____, _____, _____
dislike: _____, _____

> **Match examples 1–2 with rules a–b.**
>
> 1 *I prefer wearing scruffy clothes.*
> 2 *Dressing up is really good fun.*
>
> You can use the *-ing* form:
> a) as the subject of a sentence.
> b) after certain verbs (e.g. *like, don't mind*).
>
> Find two more examples of each type in the texts.
>
> ....
> ....
>
> **Remember!**
> We say *I would like + to + infinitive*.
> Compare these examples.
> *I would like to go to a salsa club tonight.*
> *I like dancing salsa.*
>
> *See Reference Guide, p. 16.*
> *See Workbook, p. 72, exs 1–2.*

Practice

Complete the sentences with the *-ing* form of these verbs.

buy	dress up	look	pay
put	~~put on~~	wear	work

1 <u>Putting on</u> make-up is a waste of time.
2 I like _____ a lot of gel in my hair.
3 I'm not into _____ second-hand clothes in markets. I prefer new things.
4 I love my job. _____ as a model is fun.
5 I adore _____ in strange clothes.
6 I have a shave every day. I can't stand _____ scruffy.
7 _____ a suit and tie is uncomfortable, but I need to look smart at work.
8 I don't mind _____ more to have comfortable shoes.

Speaking & Writing

Changes of look

1 Have you ever changed your image or look (haircut, glasses, different clothes)?

> **Useful language**
> When I was a teenager …
> … I used to wear more casual clothes.
> … I didn't use to have long hair.

2 What do you know about the people in the photos? What are they famous for?

3 In pairs, write sentences about how their looks have changed. Describe the photos and any other looks you can remember.

EXAMPLE: David Beckham used to have longer hair but then he changed his image. Now he looks …

United colours

Vocabulary

Clothes nouns and adjectives

1 Match the words (1–20) with the pictures (a–t).

1	belt r	11	skirt
2	blouse	12	socks
3	boots	13	suit
4	boxers	14	sweater
5	cap	15	tie
6	coat	16	tights
7	fleece	17	tracksuit
8	high heels	18	trainers
9	scarf	19	trousers
10	shirt	20	t-shirt

2 Put the clothes into these categories.

singular	plural
belt	trousers

upper body	lower body	both
fleece	socks	suit

3 Put these adjectives into categories: *materials*, *colour* or *age*.

> black   cotton   green   leather   new
> old   pink   red   second-hand   silk

EXAMPLE: colour – black

Language focus

Adjective order

This sentence shows the rules for adjective order. Complete the rules with the categories from Vocabulary exercise 3.

An old black leather jacket.

The order is: 1 ...., 2 ...., 3 ....

See Reference Guide, p. 16.
See Workbook, pp. 72–3, exs 3–5.

Practice

Put these clothes descriptions into the correct order.

1 a plastic belt red   a red plastic belt
2 shoes new brown leather
3 a white t-shirt cotton
4 a sweater green second-hand
5 a dress blue silk new
6 boots leather pink

Listening & Writing

1  🎧 **11.3** Listen to a person describing a favourite item of clothing. What is it?

2 Listen again and answer the questions.

  1 What is it like?   4 How often does she wear it?
  2 Where did she buy it?   5 What does it remind her of?
  3 How long has she had it?

3 Write a description of a favourite item of clothing and read it to your partner. Can he / she guess what you are describing?

> **Useful language**
>
> It's made of …   It reminds me of …
> I've had it since / for …

Speaking & Reading

1 Answer the questions. Which colour:

  1 do you normally prefer for clothes?
  2 do you never wear?
  3 would you choose to decorate your bedroom?
  4 make you feel angry, calm or depressed?

2 Look at the colour chart and put the eight colours in order of preference. Be spontaneous!

3 Compare your answers with your partner's. Turn to page 123. Analyse your partner's personality.

> EXAMPLE: Your favourite colour was green. This means …
> Your least favourite colour was yellow …

4 What adjectives were used to describe your partner's character? Are the adjectives positive, negative or neutral?

Language focus
The infinitive

> Match the examples (1–4) with the rules (a–b).
>
> 1 *You find it difficult to relate to other people.*
> 2 *You need to be more ambitious.*
> 3 *You are happy to live this way.*
> 4 *You plan to do great things.*
>
> You can use *to* + infinitive:
> a) after certain verbs (e.g. *need, want, learn, plan*).
> b) after certain adjectives.
>
> Find six more verbs in the 'Test your personality' text on page 123 that are followed by *to* + infinitive.
>
> ....
> ....
>
> Find two more example sentences in the text in which adjectives are followed by *to* + infinitive.
>
> ....
> ....
>
> > *See Reference Guide, p. 16.*
> > *See Workbook, p. 73, exs 6–8.*

Practice

Complete the sentences with *to* + infinitive or the *-ing* form of the verb in brackets.

1 It isn't easy <u>to buy</u> (buy) clothes for somebody else.
2 _____ (choose) a tie for my father's birthday present was really hard.
3 I've decided _____ (pack) my green baseball cap. It will be useful on holiday if it's hot.
4 Who are you planning _____ (invite) to the party?
5 I enjoy _____ (wear) second-hand clothes.
6 I would like _____ (spend) more money on clothes.

Fashion tribes

Vocabulary
Street styles

1 Match the fashion tribes (1–7) with the photos (a–g).

1 clubber   5 goth
2 headbanger   6 rasta
3 hippy   7 skater
4 punk

2 Which fashion tribes do you associate with the following? Some items can go with more than one fashion tribe.

EXAMPLE: baggy jeans – skater

baggy jeans   baseball caps   black clothes   body piercing
denim jackets   dreadlocks   dyed hair   ecstasy   ethnic clothes
incense sticks   long hair   marijuana   mohicans   sandals
silver jewellery   tattoos   tight jeans   tight t-shirts   trainers

3 Answer the questions.

1 What type of music do you associate with these fashion tribes?
2 What do you think of the people who like these musical styles?
3 Is there any 'look' associated with the music you listen to?

Listening

1 🎧 11.4 Listen to Brian, Jodie and Liz talking about their favourite music. Match them with the fashion tribes on page 102.

2 Listen again and complete the table.

	Favourite groups / DJs	Reasons they like it	Misconceptions
Brian			
Jodie			that we are hooligans, criminals
Liz	Moby / Jeff Mills		

Reading & Speaking

1 How important is your look? How much money do you spend on clothes? Do you think you are a fashion victim?

2 Complete the questionnaire. Compare your answers with your partner.

3 Turn to page 123. Calculate your partner's score and read the description. Do you think it is true? Does your partner agree?

Writing
Class survey

In pairs, write three multiple-choice questions for a class survey. Choose from these topics, or think of your own.

> clothes shops   designers
> models   bars / clubs

EXAMPLE:

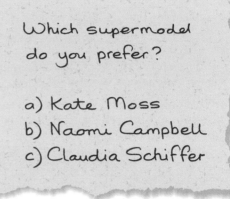

Which supermodel do you prefer?

a) Kate Moss
b) Naomi Campbell
c) Claudia Schiffer

Ask other students your questions and note their answers. Report the results to the class. Were there any surprises?

Are you a fashion victim?

1 Do you ever buy designer clothes?
  a) Only for a very special occasion.
  b) Never. It's a complete waste of money.
  c) Quite often. The quality and design are worth the extra cost.

2 Would you ever pierce your belly button?
  a) Maybe, but it would be really painful.
  b) Why not? It would probably look great.
  c) No way. I'm not into self-mutilation.

3 Would you ever have a tattoo on your shoulder?
  a) Yes. It would be cool.
  b) No, not if it was a permanent one. I would get bored of it.
  c) No. I really hate tattoos.

4 Do you ever buy second-hand clothes?
  a) No. I think it's horrible to wear other people's things.
  b) Only if it was something I couldn't find new.
  c) Yes. You can find some real bargains in the markets.

5 Where do you normally buy your clothes?
  a) My parents buy my clothes for me.
  b) In exclusive fashion boutiques.
  c) In department stores and chain stores.

6 How often do you change your winter wardrobe?
  a) Every year.
  b) Never. I've been wearing the same winter clothes for years.
  c) Every two or three years.

7 Have you ever dyed your hair?
  a) No. I like my hair colour just as it is.
  b) Yes, but only as a joke.
  c) Yes. I love to change my look!

8 Would you ever be a member of a fashion tribe?
  a) No. I am an individual and would never be a clone.
  b) Maybe. It depends on the style.
  c) I am already!

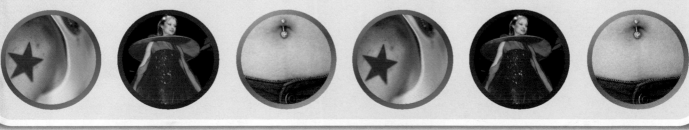

Dressing up

Speaking & Listening

1 Discuss these questions.

  1 Have you ever dressed up as a woman / man? When?

  2 What would you wear on these occasions?

> a birthday party   Carnival   New Year's Eve
> a stag / hen night   a wedding

2 (11.5) Listen to Mari, Rod and Antonia talking about dressing up. Answer the questions.

  1 What clothes did they dress up in?

  2 Who did they dress up as?

  3 For what occasion?

The Real Thing: *stuff*

1 (11.6) Listen and complete the sentences.

  1 A lot of people dressed up as famous people _____ _____.

  2 We put on blond wigs and make up and silk stockings – you know, the typical Marilyn _____.

  3 I wore this white suit and huge sunglasses _____ _____ _____ _____.

2 Does the word *stuff* make a sentence more or less specific? How would you say *and stuff* in your language?

3 (11.7) Listen and answer the questions.

  1 What are the speakers doing? Where are they?

  2 What does *stuff* refer to in each case?

4 Work in pairs. Turn to Reference Guide, page 61. Look at transcript 11.7 and continue each conversation. Use the word *stuff*.

EXAMPLE:

A: ... The car isn't big enough for all this stuff you've bought.

B: Well, we can't leave it here.

A: OK. I'll phone Mark and ask him to take some stuff in his car ...

TAKEAWAY ENGLISH: *Clothes shopping*

3 Put this conversation into the correct order.

SHOP ASSISTANT:	How would you like to pay?
CUSTOMER:	Yes, please. I'm looking for a winter coat.
SHOP ASSISTANT:	No, no ... I think it fits you really well.
CUSTOMER:	Fine. I'll take it.
SHOP ASSISTANT:	Certainly, madam.
CUSTOMER:	OK. Can I try it on?
1 – SHOP ASSISTANT:	Can I help you, madam?
CUSTOMER:	I don't think it's big enough for me.
SHOP ASSISTANT:	It's in the sale – 80 euros.
CUSTOMER:	Really? How much is it then?
SHOP ASSISTANT:	Fine. I'll just put it in a bag for you.
CUSTOMER:	Credit card.
SHOP ASSISTANT:	This one will suit you, I think.

(11.10) Listen and check.

4 Find sentences in the conversation in exercise 3 that mean:

1 I think it's too small for me.
2 I think it's exactly the right size for you.
3 I think this one will look good on you.

1 (11.8) Listen and match the conversations (1–3) with the pictures (a–d). You will not need one of the pictures. What problem does each customer have?

2 Complete the sentences with phrasal verbs.

1 Excuse me. Can I _____ these shoes, please?
2 They're not big enough. I can't even _____ them _____.
3 When I _____ them _____ at home, I realised they didn't suit me at all.
4 OK, why don't you _____ those _____ and try these?

(11.9) Listen and check.

5 Act out two dialogues.

Student A (customer)	Student B (shop assistant)
1 You want to buy a new suit / dress for work – something smart but not too expensive.	Everything really smart is quite expensive. Encourage the customer to spend more.
2 You want to return an unwanted gift – a sweater that your grandmother bought you.	You are not happy to take back the sweater. It looks dirty.

Useful language

Customer	Shop Assistant
I'd like / I'm looking for ...	Certainly / Of course.
Can I try it on?	Just a moment.
Is it OK if I return this?	Here you are.
I'll take it.	It really suits you.
It's too small / not big enough.	It fits you really well.

12 Alternatives

- Supposition: *could, might, may, must, can't*
- Forms of transport
- *get* + preposition
- *-ed / -ing* adjectives
- /juː/ & /ə/
- Future plans

Car culture

Vocabulary
Forms of transport

1 Which of these statements do you most agree with?

1 I couldn't live without a car.
2 A car is useful but not essential.
3 I think a car would improve my life.
4 I'm not at all interested in owning a car.

2 Look at the photos. Which of the cars do you prefer? Why?

3 What alternative forms of transport are shown in the pictures below? Match the words (1–8) with the pictures (a–h).

1 bike h   2 bus   3 micro-scooter
4 moped   5 motorbike   6 rollerblades
7 skateboard   8 the underground

Which do you like travelling on? Why? Can you think of any other alternative forms of transport?

Listening & Vocabulary

1 (12.1) Which form of transport do Geert, Ray, Claudia and Donna talk about?

EXAMPLE: Geert – bike

2 Listen again and answer the questions.

1 How long have they used this form of transport?
2 Why is it ideal for them?
3 Are there any disadvantages?

3 Complete these sentences from the recording with *get* and the correct preposition.

1 As soon as I <u>get on</u> my bike I feel free.
2 I can _____ work on them in about fifteen minutes.
3 I can _____ quickly and it's a great form of exercise.
4 You can _____ your board when you like and walk for a bit.
5 The best way to _____ this city is on a moped.
6 You can _____ A to B really quickly.

(12.2) Listen and check.

4 Look again at the sentences in exercise 3. What does *get* mean in each one? How would you translate it?

Try the internet activities for this unit at www.webframework.net.

Speaking & Reading

1 In pairs, make a list of the advantages and disadvantages of driving a car.

EXAMPLE:

Advantages	Disadvantages
Very convenient	Slow in traffic jams

2 Read what two people think about cars. Look at your list and tick the advantages and disadvantages that they mention. Do they mention any others?

3 Who do you agree with?

4 Find words and expressions in the text that mean the same as these.

Johnny's text
1 not enough
2 contamination
3 inventions that make cars better

Amanda's text
4 not able to move
5 a line of slow-moving cars
6 continuous
7 irritates

Song

🎧 *Driving in my car*. See resource sheet 12A.

Cars - curse or craze?

Johnny Watson, 30

It is very easy to criticise cars — they pollute, they cause accidents, and so on. But what really are the alternatives? Nobody wants to travel in a slow, smelly old bus when you can relax in the comfort of your

own car. In most countries, the public transport system is inadequate, expensive and inefficient — and anyway, cities today are designed to meet drivers' needs, with fast roads and car parks everywhere. The car industry also provides thousands of jobs. Our roads are getting safer and more efficient every year, and our cars are causing less pollution because of lead-free petrol and other technological improvements. What's the problem?

Amanda Rees, 43

I am much happier now that I don't have my car. I used to spend an hour stuck in a traffic jam each morning and that made me angry and irritable for the rest of the day. I was so stressed! The worst thing about cars, though, is the number of accidents. Did you know that somebody dies in a road accident in the UK every two and a half hours? Another thing I hate is the way that road building is destroying the countryside. Finally, I would love to live without that constant traffic noise coming through the window. In fact, I think it's the noise that bothers me most.

Lifestyles

Reading

1 Look at the photos and headline. What do you think the article is about?

2 Read the text and answer the questions.

1 What are they protesting about?
2 Why is their protest important to them?
3 Do they think their protest will be successful?

3 Who do you sympathise with most? Why?

THE YOUNG AND ANGRY: *in their own words*

A TREE DWELLER

Noah Rose, 29, is living in a treehouse to protest about a new road which the local council is planning to build.

'Sometimes you can get a bit bored of living in a treehouse. I mean, you don't have any of the basic things that you're used to. I'm here because I really feel that this road should not be built. It will just add to pollution and destroy some beautiful countryside. I know we'll succeed in the end – I'm sure we can beat the Department of Transport. Who needs more roads anyway?'

A SQUATTER

Nancy Barrett, 23, lives in a squat in New Cross Road. The police want to evict her and other squatters from the houses in the area.

'We have tied ourselves to the house, so the police can't move us out. They've got no right. This house has been empty for years and nobody owns it. We live here peacefully and don't do any harm to anyone. We don't believe in capitalism or consumerism, and that's why this protest is important. A home is a home and you shouldn't have to be grateful to the banks for that. Whatever happens, I know we'll have to leave in the end. It's depressing but that's how it is – the police always win.'

Vocabulary

-ed / -ing adjectives

1 Look at these sentences from the text.

1 Sometimes you can get a bit **bored**.
2 It's **depressing** but that's how it is.
3 Sometimes I get quite **frightened** about that.

Which adjectives, -ed or -ing, refer to:

a) what a person feels?
b) what a situation is?

2 Find other examples of -ed / -ing adjectives in the texts.

3 Complete the sentences with these adjectives. There may be more than one option.

> annoyed   ~~appalled~~   disappointed   disgusting
> exhausted   frightening   interesting   surprising

1 I was <u>appalled</u> when I heard that the police had killed one of the protesters.
2 The arguments for and against capitalism are very _____.
3 The way animals are tortured in these laboratories is _____.
4 I was really _____ with the police for trying to evict us. They had no right!
5 The decision to stop building the road is so _____ – we didn't expect to win our campaign!
6 It was _____ when they threw a brick through our window.
7 Of course I'm _____ that our protest hasn't been successful.
8 We were _____ after marching all day through the streets.

🎧 **12.4** Listen and check.

AN ANIMAL LOVER

Diane Hoyle, 24, has camped outside a well-known laboratory for the last four nights.

'I'm here because I'm an animal lover. Inside this building, scientists are experimenting on cats, guinea pigs and hamsters to test out beauty products. It's crazy that our society allows this torture. It's scandalous, in fact. Some people in our movement have taken violent action; they have attacked people and even put bombs in labs. Sometimes I get quite frightened about that – I don't agree with those tactics. We have to get our message across peacefully, but I'm sure we will succeed in the end. It's interesting how much support we're getting from the general public.'

Listening

🔊(12.5) Listen to John and Margaret talking about the demonstrators in the text. Answer the questions.

1 Who does John sympathise with? What about Margaret?
2 Who do they both disagree with? Why?
3 What does John say about protests and demonstrations in general?
4 Why does Margaret admire protestors?

The Real Thing: *actually, to be honest, in fact*

1 What does the word *actually* mean?

a) at the present time b) in reality
c) immediately

2 🔊(12.6) Listen and complete the sentences.

1 _____, I sympathised with some more than others.
2 _____, I was thinking of giving them some money.
3 _____, a lot of them come from quite rich families.
4 _____, I think it's really good what they're doing.
5 … because, _____, we never do anything, do we?

Where do *actually*, *to be honest* and *in fact* appear in the sentence? What word sometimes appears before them? How would you translate these expressions?

Speaking

Talk about news stories that have affected you. Choose from this list. Try to use *-ed / -ing* adjectives and the Real Thing phrases.

> a demonstration   an election   a pop star
> a sports event   a terrorist attack   a TV celebrity
> a TV programme   a war

EXAMPLE: A: That earthquake in Turkey was appalling.
B: Yes, actually I feel frightened about going there on holiday now.

Pronunciation
/juː/ *student* and /ə/ *study*

1 Put the words into the correct column.

argue   beautiful   computer   future   hunt
number   public   reduce   reduction   result
schedule   student   study   stupid   subject

/juː/	/ə/
student	study

🔊(12.7) Listen and check.

2 🔊(12.8) Listen and repeat these sentences.

1 In the future, studying computer science will become very important.
2 We argued a lot about the results.
3 There has been a reduction in the number of students for this subject.

Futures

Speaking & Reading

1 Look at these pictures of how previous generations imagined the future. What do they show? Have any of the predictions come true?

2 What will the world be like in 2050? Match the topics (1–6) with the predictions (a–f).

1 space travel
2 currency
3 wars
4 geography
5 marriage
6 natural disasters

a) There won't be so many, but there will be more terrorism instead.
b) There will just be one all over the world, so life will be easier.
c) There will be a lot more because of global warming.
d) At last, we will discover life on other planets.
e) Nations will break up into smaller units.
f) This won't exist. Children will take only their mother's name.

3 Make your own predictions on the same topics. Then answer the questions.

1 What do you find exciting about the future?
2 What do you find frightening about it?
3 Are you optimistic or pessimistic about the future? Why?

> **Useful language**
>
> I think there will be more / fewer (wars) ...
> Everyone will (travel) more ...
> I'm excited / frightened about the future because ...

4 Read the text. In pairs, answer the questions.

1 According to the text, what will pet computers do for us in 2050?
   EXAMPLE: They will choose our clothes.
2 What does citizen KYZ606 like about his world? What does he dislike?
   He likes: doing nothing at work, ...
   He dislikes: ...

5 Discuss these questions.

1 What is the best summary of this vision of the future?
   a) Life is great fun because computers do the boring things for us.
   b) Life is a bit boring because we are controlled by computers.
   c) Life is out of control and dangerous because computers are in charge.
2 How close to reality do you think this vision is? Which aspects do you think are believable?
3 How much of our lives are already controlled by machines and computers? How much do they know about us?

Big Brother

1950s vision of a future town

2050 - A DAY IN THE LIFE OF CITIZEN KYZ606 AND HIS PET COMPUTER DANIEL

Friday

8.00 When I wake up, my pet computer, Daniel, smiles at me and says 'Good morning.' He makes me a coffee and chooses my 'look' for the day.

9.00 At the office again. I want sunshine today so Daniel changes the lighting and air conditioning to create a sunny day. It's great here, because I don't have to think – the computers do everything. While Daniel organises my schedule, I talk to friends on my mobile videophone.

11.30 At the gym. My computer knows exactly what I need to do. I don't like doing so much exercise, but Daniel says I'll have a heart attack at the age of 53 if I don't.

13.00 Lunch in the office restaurant. We press some buttons on the food-ordering machine, and the pills arrive quickly through a hole in the table. Everything tastes really good today.

13.30 Back in the office, there's nothing to do so I take a nap. Daniel will wake me up when I've had enough sleep.

16.00 Daniel has woken me up, but there's no work to do so I do a bit of shopping online. I love shopping. Daniel helps me find a shirt that will look good at the party tonight. He really knows what I like.

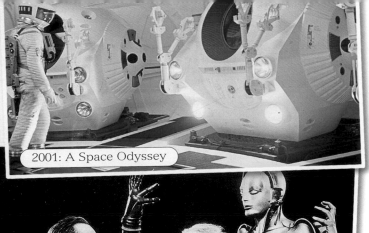

2001: A Space Odyssey

Metropolis

Writing

A diary

Work in pairs. Continue citizen KYZ606's diary for the next day. Use these notes to help you.

Saturday
9.00 – wake up
10.00 – buy food at online supermarket
11.00 – ask Daniel to clean the flat
16.00 – play online tennis
21.00 – see a film

19.00 Back at home, I watch a football match, although it's not very exciting because Daniel tells me the result before the end. He does that with films as well – I get really annoyed with him.

21.00 Party in full swing. As soon as I arrive, Daniel chooses me a partner who will be compatible. She seems very nice. I order another whisky and a red warning light goes on – I am drinking too much again!

23.00 Time for bed. Daniel prepares my pyjamas and my dreams for the night. I think I would prefer to dream on my own, but anyway ... It's been a good day ... I think!

Listening

1 (12.9) Listen to two people discussing what life will be like in 2050. What positive and negative aspects do they mention?

2 (12.10) Listen and complete the sentences.
1 Information technology _____ become the most important thing.
2 People _____ work from home more.
3 There _____ be more unemployment.
4 Doctors _____ find a cure for cancer.
5 There _____ be life out there somewhere.

Language focus

Supposition: *could, might, may, must, can't*

We use modal verbs to speculate about the future and the present. Look at the examples and complete the rules.

*People **could** / **might** / **may** work from home more.*
*There **must** be life out there somewhere.*
*There **can't** be life on Mars – lots of scientists have looked, but no one has found anything.*

We use .... when we think something is certain in the present or the future.
We use .... when we think something is impossible in the present.
We use ...., ... and .... when we think something is possible in the present or the future.

Translate an example with *must*, *can't* and *might / could / may* into your language.

....
....
....

Turn to Reference Guide, page 63, and look at transcript 12.9. Can you find other ways of speculating about the future?

See Reference Guide, p. 17.
See Workbook, p. 78, exs 1–4.

Practice

1 Do you think these things are certain, possible or impossible in the future? Complete the sentences with *will, won't, might, may* or *could*.
1 English _____ be everyone's first language.
2 The hole in the ozone layer _____ get bigger.
3 A film star _____ be the world's richest person.
4 People _____ live longer.
5 Terrorism _____ become more common.
6 They _____ discover a cure for cancer.

2 Look at the use of the definite article *the* in the sentences above. Where is it missing? Why? Is there a definite article in your language?

See Reference Guide, p. 17.
See Workbook, p. 79, exs 5–6.

Modal verbs: Try exs 1–6 on your CD-Rom. **111**

Big ideas

Speaking

1 Match the buildings (1–4) with the photos above (a–d) and the descriptions (i–iv).

1 The Guggenheim Museum, Bilbao
2 The Pompidou Centre, Paris
3 The Sydney Opera House
4 The Petronas Towers, Kuala Lumpur

i This is a building turned inside out. Water and electricity are carried along brightly coloured pipes, visible all over the building.

ii At 451 metres, this is the world's tallest building. Its 88 floors cost $1.2 billion to build.

iii Its roof looks like a collection of shells. For many years it was considered impossible to build. First designed in 1956, it was finally finished in 1973 with the help of computers.

iv It has glass walls in the shape of a ship, covered in thin 'fish scales' of titanium.

2 Discuss these questions.

1 Which of the buildings in the photos do you like most? Why?
2 What is the most emblematic building in your city / town? Why is it famous? Do you like it?
3 Are there any new buildings you particularly like / dislike?

3 Look at the photos below. What are these strange buildings for? Match the buildings (1–6) with the photos (a–f).

1 bus shelter f   4 sauna
2 meditation shelter   5 storytelling pavilion
3 public toilets   6 water tower

Useful language

Building d **might** be a sauna because it is made of wood.
Building e **can't** be a water tower because it is the wrong shape.

Reading

1 Have you ever lived in a caravan? What are the advantages and disadvantages, do you think?

2 Look at the photos below. What do the 'houses' have in common?

3 Read the texts and answer the questions.

1 How are the houses erected?
2 What are they made of?
3 What are they for?
4 Which is the more practical? Why?
5 Which would you prefer to live in? Why?

FUTURE HOMES

BASIC HOUSE

Architect: *Martín Ruíz de Azua, Spain*

This is a very basic house with only one room, and it is so portable that it fits in your pocket.

The house has an interior area of 8 cubic metres and is made from metallic polyester. The fabric is gold on one side to protect against the cold and silver on the other to keep the warmth in. It is even translucent so you can look outside. It weighs only 200 grams and has to be inflated by blowing air into the fabric – a tent but without a frame.

When you don't need a house, you can let out the air and use the fabric as a blanket. Or put the house in your pocket and move on. And the best thing? It only costs $50.

MAISON-VALISE (SUITCASE HOME)

Architects: *Claire Petetin and Philippe Gregoire, Germany*

These houses are made of light, durable materials often used in sports equipment. The units are kept flat when not in use, but can be pulled out like a concertina on wheels to create a line of temporary rooms.

The architects who designed them want to change our concept of mobile homes. They don't belong only in caravan parks and green areas – they can also be used in urban areas for homeless people, immigrants and refugees, depending on the city and the situation. The only problem? Each one costs €70,000.

TAKEAWAY ENGLISH: *Future plans*

1 (12.1) Listen to three conversations about plans for the weekend. Complete the table.

	Conversation 1	Conversation 2	Conversation 3
Plans for the weekend	staying in a new hotel in Benidorm		
Possible problems		ticket in wrong name	

2 Have similar conversations in pairs.

Conversation 1

Student A: You want to visit some friends in the country, at their cottage by the sea. You want to go by train.

Student B: You think there is a train strike. It is possible that there will be a lot of people and very few trains.

Conversation 2

Student B: You're planning to go skiing this weekend. You have already booked everything.

Student A: You think that there won't be enough snow because the weather has been very warm.

Useful language

What have you got planned ...?
What are you up to ...?

I'm going to ...
I'm off to ...

There might be a problem with ...
It could be very difficult ...
There must be some way ...

Now do Unit test 12 on your CD-Rom. 113

Who speaks English?

Vox pops

■ [23:39-25:10] Watch the vox pops and answer the on-screen questions.

1 Watch again. Who says it?

1 I speak Chinese and English and a little bit of Hindi.
2 My languages are very very bad …
3 I speak Spanish, English, French and a bit of Catalan.

2 Test your memory. Complete the gaps.

ZHENG: The best way to learn a language is either to _____ to that country or make friends with people … from the country.

LUKE: _____ in love with the culture.

OLIVER: The best way to learn a language is by _____ time in that country.

JULIETA: The best way to learn a language is _____ a person from that country.

3 What other things are these people studying at the moment?

1 Michael   3 Iqbal
2 Sarah   4 Oliver

EXAMPLE: Iqbal is doing a business training course.

Before you watch

Discuss in pairs.

1 What languages do you speak? What languages would you like to learn?
2 Look at Vox pops, exercise 2. Whose opinion do you agree with most?
3 What makes a good language teacher?
4 What do you like doing most in your English class?
5 What's your favourite English word?

While you watch

Sequence 1 [25:11-26:43]

Luke Meddings teaches English to foreign students in a language school in West London.

■ Watch sequence 1 and answer the questions.

1 What do these numbers refer to? Make sentences.

1 36 Luke is 36 years old. 2 1987 3 8.30 4 3 hours 5 12.00

2 Did Luke like teaching when he started? Why / Why not?

3 What does he like about teaching?

Sequence 2 [26:44-28:04]

■ Watch the sequence and answer the questions.

1 Complete the missing information.

Name: Mauricio
Nationality: _____
Job: _____

Name: John
Nationality: _____
Job: _____

Name: Stella
Nationality: Slovakian
Job: _____

Name: Sora
Nationality: _____
Job: _____

Name: Marcela
Nationality: _____
Job: nanny

2 Answer the questions.

1 How does John help in the school?
2 What does Sora love?
3 Why does Mauricio do a different job to his usual job?

Sequence 3 [28:05-29:59]

■ [28:05-29:17] Watch part 1 of sequence 3 and answer the questions.

1 Why do the students like living in London? Match the names with the reasons.

1 Stella   a) museums
2 Mauricio   b) parks
3 John   c) multicultural mix of people
4 Marcela   d) architecture

2 ⬛ **[29:18-29:59] Now watch the rest of sequence 3. What do Luke's students say about him? Complete the gaps.**

STELLA: He's very _____, we are doing a lot of _____, speaking, and it's kind of relax _____.

JOHN: I like the way he teach because it's very _____ ...

MARCELA: He's _____. I enjoy a lot the classes with him. I ... we practise a lot of speaking, we speak a lot in the classes and it's _____.

3 **Correct the four mistakes in red that the students make in exercise 2.**

Sequence 4 [30:00-30:41]

⬛ **Watch the sequence and answer the questions.**

1 **Luke is talking about what he is doing now and his future plans. Tick the verbs that he uses.**

enjoy   finish   play   prefer
start✓   work   write

2 **Match the verbs you ticked above with the phrases below, to make sentences about Luke.**

1 travelling
2 a book for students
3 talking at conferences
4 a couple of books

Watch the whole DVD again and answer the on-screen questions.

After you watch

1 **Can you remember? Close your books and describe the five students, Stella, Mauricio, Marcela, John, and Sora.**

What other information can you remember about them?

2 **Circle Stella and Mauricio's favourite words.**

STELLA: naturally, actually, intellectually, virtually

MAURICIO: enjoyable, comfortable, lovable, vegetable

3 **Practise saying the words in exercise 2. How many syllables does each word have? Can you think of other words that end in -ally or -able?**

World culture:
Talking in circles

1 Read the text and match the countries below to the circles.

Argentina   Australia   Belgium   Canada   Ghana
India   Ireland   Jamaica   Kenya   Nigeria   Portugal
Puerto Rico   Singapore   South Africa   Spain
Switzerland   Thailand   United States   Zimbabwe

The way English has spread around the world can be presented in three concentric circles. In **inner circle** countries, English is spoken as a first language. In **outer circle** countries, English plays an important role as one of several official languages, because of colonial links with Britain. In **expanding circle** countries, English is taught as a foreign language.

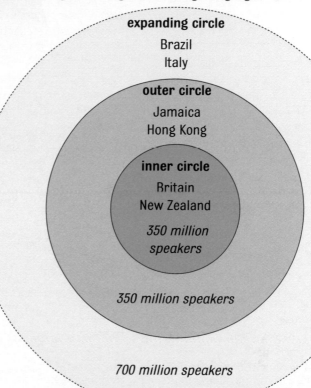

expanding circle
Brazil
Italy

outer circle
Jamaica
Hong Kong

inner circle
Britain
New Zealand

350 million speakers

350 million speakers

700 million speakers

Where would you place your country?

2 These countries all have high numbers of speakers of English as a second language. Match the countries with the figures.

1 Hong Kong	**a)**	37 million
2 India	**b)**	10 million
3 Nigeria	**c)**	36.4 million
4 South Africa	**d)**	43 million
5 The Philippines	**e)**	1.8 million

Let's talk

Discuss the questions.

1 What has been the best and the worst thing about learning English for you?
2 How many native speakers of English do you know? How many non-native speakers of English do you know? Who do you find it easiest to understand?
3 Which English-speaking country would you most like to visit? Why?
4 How do you hope your English will help you in the future?

Flashback 4

Vocabulary & Speaking

1 a Complete the crossword. Look at Unit 11 if you need help.

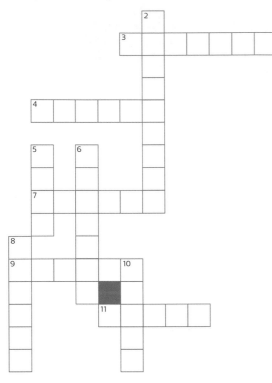

Across

3 Shoes, belts and sometimes trousers are made of this. (7)

4 Jeans and a sweatshirt are examples of _____ clothes. (6)

7 If you follow the latest fashions, you're _____. (6)

9 Levi, Lacoste and Calvin Klein are all _____. (6)

11 The opposite of tight for clothes. (5)

Down

2 Rings, bracelets and necklaces are examples of this. (9)

5 If an item of clothing is the right size for you, it _____. (4)

6 Another way to say jumper or jersey. (7)

8 A shirt designed for a woman. (6)

10 Men often wear a suit and tie when they want to look _____. (5)

b Write definitions to describe other clothes and street style vocabulary in Unit 11. Swap them with a partner.

c Work in pairs. Make a list of five different social situations. What would you wear?

EXAMPLE: *If I met my boyfriend's parents, I would wear smart trousers.*

2 a Choose the correct form of the adjective.

1 It's really **bored / boring**. I used to be **interested / interesting** when I was a student, but nobody talks about real issues any more. Everyone just says what will get them more votes. I find it very **disappointed / disappointing**.

2 I absolutely love it. A lot of people get **bored / boring** but I think it's really **excited / exciting**. You don't have to buy anything. It's fun just to go around looking at what's new. It's inspiring!

3 I hate them. I've been **frightened / frightening** of them since I was a child. The city where I live is full of them, and it's really **annoyed / annoying** because people let them run anywhere. And then they use the pavement as a toilet. That's really **disgusted / disgusting**!

b What topic is each person talking about? Choose from the topics below.

dogs	fashion	politics	shopping
	squatters	teenagers	

c Write what you think about one of the other topics. Read it to a partner. Can they guess what you're talking about?

Pronunciation

1 a Circle the underlined letter that is pronounced differently.

1 cul<u>t</u>ure fu<u>t</u>ure ac<u>t</u>ually <u>ch</u>aos <u>ch</u>at adven<u>t</u>ure

2 na<u>t</u>ure <u>ch</u>ief <u>ch</u>urch <u>ch</u>ocolate <u>ch</u>emist <u>ch</u>ild

3 pa<u>ss</u>ion fa<u>sh</u>ion sweat<u>sh</u>irt op<u>t</u>ion plea<u>s</u>ure Engli<u>sh</u>

4 televi<u>s</u>ion ca<u>s</u>ual trea<u>s</u>ure <u>s</u>pecial unu<u>s</u>ual occa<u>s</u>ion

5 <u>p</u>unctual n<u>u</u>mber res<u>u</u>lt st<u>u</u>dent st<u>u</u>dy inc<u>o</u>me

6 red<u>u</u>ction bea<u>u</u>tiful st<u>u</u>pid comp<u>u</u>ter n<u>e</u>w arg<u>ue</u>

b (F4.1) Listen and check.

Listening

1 a  *(F4.2)* Listen to the conversation and make a note of Eric and Vanessa's plans for the summer.

	Vanessa	Eric
Where, when and for how long?	Disneyland, Paris	
Possible problems and solutions		

b Make a list of the structures you can use to talk about future plans.

EXAMPLE: I'm off to …

c Work in pairs. Ask and answer questions about your summer plans. Use your list.

Language focus

1 Work in pairs. Write four sentences using adverbs from Unit 10. Cut up the sentences and give them to your partner. Can he / she re-order them?

2 a Complete the definitions with *who*, *which* or *where*.

1 A person _____ lives in a foreign country. (Unit 10)
2 The cupboard _____ you keep your clothes. (Unit 11)
3 A small shop _____ sells expensive, trendy clothes. (Unit 11)
4 A person _____ has dreadlocks and likes reggae music. (Unit 11)
5 A party _____ women organise for their women friends before they get married. (Unit 11)
6 A person _____ lives for free in a house that isn't his / hers. (Unit 12)

b Find the words which match the definitions.

3 a Write the correct form of the verb in brackets.

1 Do you like _____ (shop) for clothes?
2 Would you like _____ (live) in another country?

3 _____ (travel) can make you a more open person. Do you agree?
4 What is it about English that you find easiest _____ (learn)?
5 Do you need _____ (use) English now in your daily life?
6 Is there any type of music that you can't stand _____ (listen) to?
7 Is it really worth _____ (go) to university?
8 Is it difficult _____ (find) work where you live?

b In pairs, ask and answer the questions.

4 a *(F4.3)* Listen to two students talking about the note below. Who is Laura?

> Laura González

b Listen again. Which expressions mean:

a) It's possible. b) It's impossible. c) It's certain.
a) It could be …

You *choose!*

1 a Work in groups. Look at Units 1–12 and write down ten discussion points on pieces of card.

EXAMPLE: Life is better as an ex-pat.
The internet is one of the best inventions of the 20th century.

b Take turns to pick up a card. Talk for two minutes about the issue. The person with the strongest argument wins.

OR

2 a Work in pairs. Write six words that express your life now or your future plans.

EXAMPLE: 1) gardens

b Swap lists. Try to guess the meaning of the words.

EXAMPLE: 1) 'I think you might want to buy a house with a garden in the future.'
'Sorry, no. Try again!'

Communication bank

Unit 1

London: Multicultural capital of the world
(pages 8–9)

Student A

1 Complete the questions.

A India
1 When did most people from India arrive in London?
The 1950s and 60s.
2 How often … ?
Every two weeks.

B Greece
1 In 'Little Athens' how long … ?
All night.
2 What kind of food … ?
Cakes and pastries.

C West Africa
1 What sort … ?
Yams and different types of rice.
2 Which area … ?
South-east London.

2 Complete the questions with the correct question words.

D China
1 Who were the first arrivals?
2 _____ can you buy in Chinatown?

E The Caribbean
1 _____ did people from the Caribbean islands arrive in the UK? (date)
2 _____ does the Notting Hill Carnival take place? (date)

F Ireland
1 _____ does the Irish community come from?
2 _____ perform in pubs all over the city?

3 Answer your partner's questions on texts A–C. Do you have the same questions?

4 Now read your partner the questions on texts D–F. Do you have the same question words? Write down the answers.

Unit 3

Takeaway English: A job interview
(page 29)

Student A

You are looking for people who are suitable for these jobs.

TAXI DRIVER NEEDED URGENTLY!

Requirements:

- Own car
- Clean driving licence
- Five years experience as a driver
- Able to work night shift one day a week

Good conditions for the right person.

LIFEGUARD / CLEANER

needed for Bellevue hotel swimming pool (June–September)

Requirements:
- Age 18–35
- Proficient swimmer
- Some life-saving experience necessary
- Able to work weekends and overtime in summer season

Responsibilities:
- Clean pool and garden area
- Enforce rules and regulations in pool area

LOCAL CITY GUIDE

Sunny Tours need a local guide for holiday season in cities around Europe.

Requirements:
- Age 21+
- Knowledge of local city's monuments
- Good level of Spanish, English and some knowledge of a third European language
- Energetic, sociable and hard-working

No previous experience is necessary.

Unit 1

Takeaway English: Giving directions

(page 13)

Student A

1 Look at the map of Madrid. Give directions from your hotel to:

a) Prado Museum   b) Atocha Station   c) Retiro Park
d) Puerta del Sol   e) Opera House

2 Look at the map of Glasgow. Ask for directions from your hotel to:

a) George Square   b) Botanical Gardens
c) Macintosh School of Art   d) Merchant City
e) Central Station

Match the places (a–e) with the numbers on the map (1–5).

Use the Useful language on page 13 to help you.

Unit 5

Takeaway English: Booking a hotel

(page 49)

Student A

1 You are the receptionist of the Hotel Belvedere. Look at the information about the hotel.

Hotel Belvedere****

Double: 85 euros (Half board)
Views of Kelvingrove Park
En suite bathroom
Full room service and mini bar
Internet connection
Satellite TV

Ideal for business people.

Answer your partner's questions.

2 Swap roles. You need a cheap hotel (around 50 euros) for the night with breakfast included. The area is not important. Find out about the Hotel Douglas.

Unit 6

Are you a junk food freak?

(page 50)

Key

Mostly As: You are incredibly resistant to the fast food invasion. Eating well is obviously important to you and you think fast food is unhealthy. But don't be too obsessed. Super-healthy eating can get boring and you should take a break from time to time. Don't feel guilty about eating that packet of chocolate biscuits – it's quite normal, you know!

Mostly Bs: You find convenience food useful because you don't always have time or energy to cook a decent meal. You shouldn't worry too much – there's nothing wrong with a sandwich or a frozen pizza when there's nothing else. Maybe you should cook a little more often, especially if you have guests. It can be very therapeutic.

Mostly Cs: You are an official fast food addict. You hate cooking, and eating healthy food is a low priority for you. You love all things American, especially if you can buy them at McDonald's. You should definitely try to eat less chocolate. But don't worry too much, because soon you'll find out that fast food is healthier than many people think!

Unit 1

London: Multicultural capital of the world
(pages 8–9)

Student B

1 Complete the questions.

D China

1 Who were the first arrivals?
Seamen. They worked on steamships.

2 What … ?
Chinese vegetables, herbal medicines and gifts.

E The Caribbean

1 When … ?
During the 1950s.

2 When … ?
Every August.

F Ireland

1 Where … ?
All over Ireland – north and south.

2 Who … ?
Irish bands and folk singers.

2 Complete the questions with the correct question words.

A India

1 When did most people from India arrive in London?

2 _____ _____ does a typical family have a curry?

B Greece

1 In 'Little Athens', _____ _____ do some of the shops stay open?

2 _____ _____ _____ food do people with a sweet tooth love?

C West Africa

1 _____ _____ _____ food do many London markets sell?

2 _____ area do a lot of Nigerians live in?

3 Now read your partner the questions on texts A–C. Do you have the same question words? Write down the answers.

4 Answer your partner's questions on texts D–F. Do you have the same questions?

Unit 3

Takeaway English: A job interview
(page 29)

Student B

You are looking for people who are suitable for these jobs.

OFFICE JUNIOR — SANTA BARBARA INSURANCE

Insurance company urgently seeks responsible office worker.

- Age 18–25
- Computer literate
- Good telephone manner
- Office experience not necessary (fast typing a bonus)
- Smart appearance
- Ideal first job

Hotel Caribe
RECEPTIONIST for Hotel Caribe

New city centre 5***** hotel requires receptionist to start immediately.

- Age 21+
- Computer literate
- Knowledge of English essential
- Able to work long shifts at night and at weekends
- Impeccable appearance

This position would suit someone wishing to gain experience in the tourist industry.

NEW JAPANESE RESTAURANT SEEKS
WAITER / BAR PERSON

Requirements:
- Age 17–22
- Open personality and polite manner
- English an advantage
- Experience in catering preferred

Responsibilities:
- Working behind the bar
- Serving tables

Salary negotiable.

We are a rapidly expanding chain. There is opportunity for fast promotion for the right person.

Unit 1

Takeaway English: Giving directions

(page 13)

Student B

1 Look at the map of Madrid. Ask for directions from your hotel to:

a) Prado Museum   b) Atocha Station   c) Retiro Park
d) Puerta del Sol   e) Opera House

Match the places (a–e) with the numbers on the map (1–5).

Use the Useful language on page 13 to help you.

2 Look at the map of Glasgow. Give directions from your hotel to:

a) George Square   b) Botanical Gardens
c) Macintosh School of Art   d) Merchant City
e) Central Station

Unit 5

Takeaway English: Booking a hotel

(page 49)

Student B

1 You are a businessman and need a room for a week. You need an internet connection for your laptop computer and full room service. Find out about the Hotel Belvedere.

2 Swap roles. You are the receptionist of the Hotel Douglas. Look at the information about the hotel.

Hotel Douglas **

Double: 65 euros *(Breakfast included)*
Views of George Square
Ensuite bathroom
Private terrace

Central location

Answer your partner's questions.

Unit 7

Are you mean with money?

(page 63)

Key

Mostly As: You're a kind and generous person. Money is not the most important thing in the world and you're happy to share it with others. Be careful not to give too much money away, however – people could take advantage of your kindness.

Mostly Bs: You're an incredibly mean person. Money is obviously the most important thing in your life and the problem is, you want it all for yourself. A word of warning: if you continue like this, you won't have many friends left. So spend a little more next time, OK?

Mostly Cs: You're quite careful with money. It's good to be responsible and someone that people can trust, but why not be a bit more extravagant at times? Don't think too much before you spend. If you see something you like, just buy it!

Unit 2

Are you a true friend?

(page 19)

Work out your score.

1	a) 10 points	b) 15 points	c) 5 points
2	a) 15 points	b) 10 points	c) 5 points
3	a) 5 points	b) 15 points	c) 10 points
4	a) 15 points	b) 5 points	c) 10 points
5	a) 5 points	b) 15 points	c) 10 points
6	a) 5 points	b) 15 points	c) 10 points

70–90 points

You are a loyal and faithful friend. You stand by your friends and help them if they have problems. But don't forget to think of yourself too!

50–70 points

You are a good friend when times are good, but you can be a bit selfish as well. Remember – a good friend is one of the most important things in life. Don't let them disappear!

30–50 points

You are a selfish person and only think about yourself. A friend for you is someone who you can use to get what you want. You should learn to think of other people or you could become a very lonely person!

Unit 9

You and your messages

(page 80)

Key

RED: You love getting messages and you answer them immediately. But without a mobile, you would be completely lost. You don't go to the cinema, because if you went, you would have to turn off your mobile and risk losing a message. Be careful – there is more to life than your mobile phone!

YELLOW: You have fun with text messages and you've developed an almost perfect relationship with your mobile. You understand the limits and the potential of text messages. If you lost your mobile tomorrow, you'd be upset but you wouldn't die!

BLUE: For you, text messages are annoying, inhuman and just a waste of time. However, when you do use your mobile, you know exactly why and the effect it will have. It's not your favourite form of communication – you would only send a text message if you didn't have any other choice.

Unit 8

Music legends

(page 71)

Can you identify the music legends and the groups they belonged to? Match them with the photos of their fans on page 71. Work in groups of three.

Student A: Read text A.
Student B: Read text B.
Student C: Read text C.

A

He was born in Liverpool in 1940 and died exactly 40 years later. He left school when he was 16 and went to Liverpool Art College. There, he formed a group called The Quarrymen. Later they changed their name and became perhaps the most popular music band of all time, with hits like *I Want To Hold Your Hand* and *A Hard Day's Night*. In the 1960s, this group dominated the music charts, having the most number one hits in rock and pop history. He was well known for his peace protests. Tragically, in 1980, he was shot dead in New York by a crazy fan. Even now, wherever you go in the world, you are still more likely to hear his group's music than any other.

B

She was born in 1950 in New Haven, Connecticut and became famous for the songs she recorded with her brother Richard. Although they didn't write their own songs, the duo became one of the most popular acts in the 70s, with hits like *We've Only Just Begun* and *Top of the World*. They developed a cult following that loved their soft, romantic music. They sold more records than anyone in the United States in that decade. She died unexpectedly at the age of 32 from a heart attack, caused by chronic anorexia. Her death opened many people's eyes to this terrible disease.

C

He was born in 1967 in Washington State. He became famous for introducing a new type of music called 'grunge' – a form of hippy punk which became a cultural phenomenon in the early 1990s. His band's songs – for example, *Smells Like Teen Spirit* and *Come As You Are* – were often dark and depressing and spoke about his difficult life. More than ten million copies of the group's first LP were sold worldwide. He developed a drug habit and was hospitalised for heroin abuse. In 1994, he committed suicide in Seattle, leaving his wife Courtney Love, also a well-known singer, and a young daughter. His untimely death has made him a popular music legend.

Unit 11

Are you a fashion victim?
(page 103)

Key

1	a) 10 points	b) 5 points	c) 15 points
2	a) 10 points	b) 15 points	c) 5 points
3	a) 15 points	b) 10 points	c) 5 points
4	a) 15 points	b) 10 points	c) 5 points
5	a) 5 points	b) 15 points	c) 10 points
6	a) 15 points	b) 5 points	c) 10 points
7	a) 5 points	b) 10 points	c) 15 points
8	a) 5 points	b) 10 points	c) 15 points

90–120 points

You are a total fashion victim. You get bored of looking at the same face in the morning. You love trying out new looks and spend a lot of money on good quality clothes. Be careful not to change your look too often – people might not even recognise you the next time they see you!

65–90 points

You don't mind dressing up for a special occasion but you don't care too much about what you wear. You sometimes like surprising people with a new outfit or unusual earrings, but in general you like casual clothes and don't take too many risks.

40–65 points

Clothes have no real importance for you. You have no interest in shopping and consider designer clothes a waste of money. You are happy with the way you look – without tattoos, piercings and strange hairstyles – and prefer people to accept you like that.

Unit 11

Test your personality
(page 101)

BLUE
Blue means you are a calm person. You are a loyal friend and enjoy being part of a group. The only problem is that you can be too easy-going – perhaps you need to be more ambitious. Blue in the last position indicates that you are unhappy at the moment and need a change in your life.

YELLOW
You are an imaginative and adventurous person. You are extremely sociable and seem to need the company of others. You have problems like everybody else but you usually try to forget about them.
Putting yellow in the last position shows that you are feeling a little shy.

PURPLE
You are a bit of a dreamer. You are shy and find it difficult to relate to other people. You usually choose to spend your spare time in your own company.
In the last position, purple indicates that you are a mature person, in control of your life.

GREEN
You are a kind and sensitive person. You love nature and the environment and you want to live a quiet life. However, you tend to be a little too serious at times – try to enjoy life more. Having green in the last place indicates that you are very stressed at the moment – learn to relax.

RED
You are a spontaneous and lively person. You love being busy and find it hard to know when to stop. You are very outgoing, so you find it easy to make friends.
In the last position, red indicates that you feel a little depressed right now. Cheer up!

BLACK
Black is the colour of protest and rebellion. You find it difficult to trust people and reject the help of others. You are happy to live this way but you can get depressed easily too.
In the last position, black means that you are generally happy with life.

ORANGE
You love being the centre of attention. You are impulsive and don't always think about the consequences of doing something. Your fun-loving personality means that you have a great social life. You are glad to be alive!
If you put orange last, you are pretending to be more confident than you feel.

PINK
You are a romantic person who is also a little idealistic, so you sometimes decide to trust the wrong people. You are adventurous and plan to do great things in the future.
In the last place, pink indicates that you worry a lot about life.

Unit 7

Advertising

(page 68)

Flashback 3

Writing & Speaking

(page 88)

Write down the following telephone dialogues.

1 You've just bought a new palmtop but there's a problem with it. You telephone Computer Zone and ask to speak to Pete Rogers, the sales assistant. He's busy. You call again later and tell him about the problem.

2 You want to borrow your friend Rosa's laptop at the weekend. You phone her but she isn't there. You leave a message with her flatmate. You call again later and ask Rosa if she can help you.

Flashback 3

Do you love the world of gossip?

(page 89)

Key

Mostly As: Yes, you love gossip. You probably know the names of royal families around the world, and the intimate details of famous people's lives.

Mostly Bs: You don't really like gossip. You prefer more serious newspapers and TV programmes to magazines and popular TV.

Mostly Cs: You don't follow the lives of famous people but you know more than you pretend. Admit it, you're a bit curious!

Irregular verbs

Infinitive	Past Tense	Participle
be	was, were	been
become	became	become
begin	began	begun
bite	bit	bitten
break	broke	broken
bring	brought	brought
build	built	built
buy	bought	bought
catch	caught	caught
choose	chose	chosen
come	came	come
cost	cost	cost
do	did	done
dream	dreamt/dreamed	dreamt/dreamed
drink	drank	drunk
eat	ate	eaten
fall	fell	fallen
feel	felt	felt
fight	fought	fought
find	found	found
fly	flew	flown
forbid	forbade	forbidden
forget	forgot	forgotten
forgive	forgave	forgiven
get	got	got/gotten (US)
give	gave	given
go	went	gone
grow	grew	grown
have	had	had
hear	heard	heard
hide	hid	hidden
hit	hit	hit
hold	held	held
hurt	hurt	hurt
keep	kept	kept
know	knew	known
lead	led	led
learn	learnt/learned	learnt/learned
leave	left	left
let	let	let
light	lit/lighted	lit/lighted
lose	lost	lost
make	made	made
meet	met	met
pay	paid	paid
put	put	put

Infinitive	Past Tense	Participle
read /riːd/	read /red/	read /red/
ride	rode	ridden
ring	rang	rung
rise	rose	risen
run	ran	run
say	said	said
see	saw	seen
sell	sold	sold
send	sent	sent
set	set	set
shake	shook	shaken
shoot	shot	shot
show	showed	shown/showed
shut	shut	shut
sing	sang	sung
sit	sat	sat
sleep	slept	slept
smell	smelt/smelled	smelt/smelled
speak	spoke	spoken
spend	spent	spent
spill	spilt/spilled	spilt/spilled
spread	spread	spread
stand	stood	stood
steal	stole	stolen
stick	stuck	stuck
stink	stank/stunk	stunk
strike	struck	struck
swear	swore	sworn
sweep	swept	swept
swell	swelled	swollen/swelled
swim	swam	swum
swing	swung	swung
take	took	taken
teach	taught	taught
tear	tore	torn
tell	told	told
think	thought	thought
throw	threw	thrown
understand	understood	understood
upset	upset	upset
wake	woke	woken
wear	wore	worn
weep	wept	wept
wet	wet/wetted	wet/wetted
win	won	won
write	wrote	written

Phonetic chart

Vowels: Monothongs

/iː/	he	/hiː/
/ɪ/	sit	/sɪt/
/e/	red	/red/
/æ/	hat	/hæt/
/ɑː/	start	/stɑːt/
/ɒ/	not	/nɒt/
/ɔː/	sport	/spɔːt/
/ʊ/	foot	/fʊt/
/uː/	shoe	/ʃuː/
/ʌ/	cup	/kʌp/
/ɜː/	bird	/bɜːd/
/ə/	father	/fɑːðə/

Vowels: Diphthongs

/eɪ/	make	/meɪk/
/aɪ/	why	/waɪ/
/ɔɪ/	boy	/bɔɪ/
/aʊ/	how	/haʊ/
/əʊ/	no	/nəʊ/
/ɪə/	beer	/bɪə/
/eə/	where	/weə/
/ʊə/	tour	/tʊə/

Semi-vowels

/j/	yes	/jes/
/w/	when	/wen/

Consonants

/p/	pen	/pen/
/b/	bad	/bæd/
/t/	ten	/ten/
/d/	dad	/dæd/
/k/	cold	/kəʊld/
/g/	girl	/gɜːl/
/m/	me	/miː/
/n/	near	/nɪə/
/ŋ/	ring	/rɪŋ/
/f/	fast	/fɑːst/
/v/	very	/verɪ/
/θ/	three	/θriː/
/ð/	father	/fɑːðə/
/tʃ/	cheese	/tʃiːz/
/dʒ/	john	/dʒɒn/
/s/	see	/siː/
/z/	zoo	/zuː/
/ʃ/	she	/ʃiː/
/ʒ/	vision	/vɪʒən/
/h/	house	/haʊs/
/l/	lot	/lɒt/
/r/	run	/rʌn/

Richmond Publishing
4 King Street Cloisters
Albion Place
London W6 0QT
United Kingdom

Published by Richmond Publishing®, 2003
© Ben Goldstein, 2003
© Santillana Educación, S.L. 2003

ISBN: 84-294-9613-0

Depósito Legal: M-2411-2004
Printed in Spain:
Palgraphic, S.A.
28970 Humanes (Madrid)

'Flashback' pages:
Gill Holley, Robert Metcalf

Design and layout:
Rob Briggs, ROARR Design

Cover Design:
Novimago, S.L.

Illustrations:
Kathy Baxendale, José Luis Gil, Pieter Lüthi, Stefanie Saile

The Publishers would like to thank all those who have given their kind permission to reproduce material for this book.

Warner Bros, 20th Century Fox, RTL2 Television, McDonalds, Adbusters Media Foundation, Luttoxica (RayBan), Jaguar Cars Ltd, Atelier Hitoshi Abe, Michael Culpepper

iT's Magazine for an extract based on 'A gap year' article (Winter, 2000); Sonia Purnell for an extract based on her article 'Kidults' (*Financial Times Magazine*, 22nd December 2001); Maya Simínovich of Magnet Comunicaciones for an adapted quiz based on 'Tu y los mensajes, como los llevas?'

Driving In My Car
Words and Music by Michael Barson
© 1982 EMI Music Publishing Ltd, London WC2H 0QY
Reproduced by permission of International Music Publications Ltd
All Rights Reserved.

I Heard It Through The Grapevine
Words and Music by Norman Whitfield and Barrett Strong
© 1966 Stone Agate Music Inc, USA
Jobete Music (UK) Ltd, London WC2H 0QY
Reproduced by permission of International Music Publications Ltd
All Rights Reserved.

Theme from "New York, New York"
Words by Fred Ebb
Music by John Kander
© 1977 EMI Catalogue Partnership, EMI Unart Catalog Inc and EMI United Partnership Ltd, USA
Worldwide print rights controlled by Warner Bros. Publications Inc/IMP Ltd
Reproduced by permission of International Music Publications Ltd
All Rights Reserved.

Every effort has been made to trace the holders of copyright, but if any omissions can be rectified, the publishers will be pleased to make the necessary arrangements.

Photographs:
A. Toril; A. Viñas; Algar; D. López; D. Lezama; F. de Madariaga; F. Ontañón; GARCIA-PELAYO /Juancho; J. Jaime; J. L. Potenciano; J. Lucas; J. M. Escudero; J. Soler; J. V. Resino; Juan M. Ruiz; Krauel; L. Agromayor; M. Catalan; O. Torres; P. Esgueva; Prats i Camps; R. Briggs; Y.Christian; PUIGDENGOLAS. FOTOGRAFIA; A.G.E FOTOSTOCK; ABB FOTÓGRAFOS; ABB FOTÓGRAFOS./F. Baixeras; ACI - ROCA-SASTRE/David Redfern/ MUSICPICTURES; THE ADVERTISING ARCHIVE U.K; BRITISH FILM INSTITUTE; COMSTOCK; CONTIFOTO; CONTIFOTO/Giuliano Bevilacqua; COVER/CORBIS SYGMA/John Van Hasselt; COVER/CORBIS SYGMA / SUNSET BOULEVARD; CONTIFOTO/FARABOLAFOTO; CONTIFOTO/ ONLINE USA INC./Andrew Shawaf; COVER/POPPERFOTO; CONTIFOTO/ PRESSE SPORTS/M. Twight / FREESTYLE / P.S.; COVER/SYGMA; COVER/SYGMA/B. Rieger-Museart, Bernard Annebicque, Daniel Giry, F. Pitchal; J. P. Laffont, Jean-Pierre Amet, Michel Setboun, O. Baumgartner, Orban, Philippe Giraud; COVER/SYGMA/VIENNAREPORT; CONTIFOTO/VANDYSTADT/Gerard Vandystadt; COVER/SLOCOMB/ PHOTOLINK/CORBIS KIPA, Ted Streshinsky;COVER/CORBIS, Photonica Europe Limit/Johner, Recoletos Grupo de Com, Peter Turnley/ CORBIS, CORBIS SYGMA, PACHA, Duomo; Kim Sayer, Rune Hellestad, Wolfgang Kaehler, COVER/Photonica Europe Limit/Christian Roth/Spoo, Roxann Arwen Mills, Ricardo Azoury, Empics, Henry Horenstein, Gregory Conraux, Jack Hutcheson, Martin Klimas, Safia Fatimi, Ryuichi Sato,Paul Vozdic, Photonica Europe Limit/Elke Hesser, Darren Robb, Brandon Harman, Dana Tezarr, Brad Wilson, Erika Kyte, Vincent Charmette, Eric Perry, Smith Richard Frank/CORBIS SYGMA; COVER/CORBIS/ Joseph Sohm; ChromoSohm Inc., Bob Rowan; Progressive Image, Hulton-Deutsch Collection, Larry Lee Photography, LWA-Stephen Welstead, Vittoriano Rastelli, Matthew Mendelsohn, Brandtner&Staedeli, Lawrence Manning, Mitchell Gerber, Michael Brennan, Franz-Marc Frei, Lynn Goldsmith, Leif Skoogfors, Karl Weatherly, Joel W. Rogers, Walter Hodges, Reed Kaestner, Marc Garanger, David Turnley, Photo B.D.V., Paul Edmondson, Ondrea Barbe, Neal Preston, Morton Beebe, Rufus F. Folkks, Leland Bobbé, Kurt Krieger, Julie Houck, Frédéric Huijbregts, Tom Nebbia, Bill Miles, Dejan Patic, Yang Liu, PACHA, Duomo; COVER/CORBIS SYGMA/ Le Segretain Pascal, SUNSET BOULEVARD, Phil Bonan/Alamo, John Van Hasselt, Hamilton Karie, Orban Thierry, Koskas David, TOUHIG SION, Tim Graham, Michael Yassukovich; CHROMA/A. Carles; DIGITALVISION; EFE; EFE/J. Martínez Espinosa; EFE/EPA PHOTO/ Ferdinand Ostrop, PRESS ASSOCIATION FILES / Laura Woolnoug; EFE/EPA PHOTO AFPI/Seth McCallister; EFE/HO REUTERS; EFE/SIPA-PRESS; EFE/SIPA-PRESS/Abril, Anmar Abd-Rabbo, Brad Rickerby, Caroline Parent, Croisille, Dalmas, De Mulder, E. Malanca, Labor, Lilo/Lucasfilm Ltd., Marcou, Michael Abramson, Peter Stumpf, Pougeoise, Richard Manin, Sichov, Steve Schneider, Tabax / Sunshine; EFE/SIPA-PRESS/GRMAN; EFE/SIPA-PRESS/SIPA; EFE/SIPA-PRESS/SIPA SPORT; EFE/SIPA-PRESS/SUNSTAR; ESTUDIO TRECE POR DIECIOCHO; EUROPA PRESS/ACTION PRESS; EUROPA PRESS/KEYSTONE; FACTEUR D'IMAGES/Fabien Malot; GETTY IMAGES/Grant V. Faint/ The Image Bank, Chad Ehlers/The Image Bank, Burke/Triolo Productiones, Christina Peters/FoodPix, Christian Lantry/Stone, Daniel Bosler/Stone, Chris Everard/Stone, Paul Webster/Stone, Mike McQueen/Stone, Joe Cornish/ Stone, The Image Bank, Luis Veiga/The Image Bank, Phil Banko/Stone, Joel Simon/Stone, Stone; IBIZA FOTOESTUDIO, S.L./R. MARTÍNEZ; HEMERA TECHNOLOGIES; INDEX/TAXI; JOHN FOXX IMAGES; JOHN BIRDSALL PHOTO LIBRARY; KEYSTONE-NEMES; LOBO PRODUCCIONES / C. SANZ; MUSEUM ICONOGRAFÍA/J. Martin; PHOTOALTO; PHOTODISC; REX FEATURES LTD; SANTILLANA USA PUBLISHING COMP; STOCKBYTE; V.O. PRESS/PHOTOEDIT/Mark Richards; IBEROAMERICANA DISTRIBUCIÓN; LVMH/TAG HEUER; MATTON-BILD © Stockbyte; PANASONIC; SERIDEC PHOTOIMAGENES CD; HEDGEROW PICTURE LIBRARY/Tew; ARCHIVO SANTILLANA.
Video stills: EFS TV Production